Academic Vocabulary Toolkit 2

Mastering High-Use Words for Academic Achievement

Dr. Kate Kinsella

Australia • Brazil • Japan • Korea • Mexico • Singapore • Spain • United Kingdom • United States

**Academic Vocabulary Toolkit 2: Mastering
High-Use Words for Academic Achievement**
Dr. Kate Kinsella

Publisher: Sherrise Roehr

Executive Editors: Carmela Fazzino-Farah
and Laura LeDrean

Developmental Editor: Maureen Sotoohi

Director of U.S. Marketing: Jim McDonough

Director, Training and Tech Marketing:
Stacy Hilliard

Director of Content and Media Production:
Michael Burggren

Content Project Manager: John Sarantakis

Manufacturing Buyer: Marybeth Hennebury

Cover Design: Page 2 LLC

Interior Design: Muse Group Inc.

Composition: Neuetype

© 2013 National Geographic Learning, a part of Cengage Learning

Library of Congress Control Number: 2011945657

ISBN-13: 978-1-111-82747-2

ISBN-10: 1-111-82747-8

National Geographic Learning
20 Channel Center Street
Boston, MA 02210
USA

Cengage Learning is a leading provider of customized learning solutions with
office locations around the globe, including Singapore, the United Kingdom,
Australia, Mexico, Brazil, and Japan.

Cengage Learning products are represented in Canada by Nelson Education, Ltd.

Visit National Geographic Learning online at **ngl.cengage.com**

Visit our corporate website at **www.cengage.com**

Printed in the United States of America
5 6 7 17 16

National Geographic Learning would like to thank the following freelancers for their contributions to this series

Jennifer Carlson

Catherine Mazur

National Geographic Learning would also like to thank the following educators for their input.

Dave Bigelman South Valley High School, Ukiah, CA

Grace Bishop Houston Community College, Richmond, TX

Blanca Bruso Clinton Public Schools, Clinton, MA

Vanessa Calderon Oxnard Union High School District, Oxnard, CA

Jackie Counts Anaheim Union High School District, Anaheim, CA

Wendy Criner Anaheim Union High School District, Anaheim, CA

Sally Gearhart Santa Rosa Junior College, Santa Rosa, CA

Janet Gordon Santa Barbara School District, Santa Barbara, CA

Jeannette Hoessel Clinton Middle School, Clinton, MA

Deborah Long Merced Union High School District, Atwater, CA

Eliza Simental San Elizario ISD, San Elizario, TX

Warren Spurrier Horace Mann Middle School, El Portal, FL

Heather Stover Paso Robles High School, Paso Robles, CA

Lisa Vallejos Paso Robles Joint Unified School District, Paso Robles, CA

Mae Lombos Wazlinski Georgia Department of Education, Atlanta, GA

A Note from the Author

Dear Scholar,

Welcome to the *Academic Vocabulary Toolkit!*

I am so excited that you are going to have the opportunity to expand your vocabulary knowledge using this interactive program. To succeed in secondary school, college, and the workplace, you will need to have a powerful command of English vocabulary. The *Academic Vocabulary Toolkit* focuses on words that are used widely across different subject areas and careers in spoken and written communication. You will need to both understand and apply these practical words while participating in discussions, writing reports, and reading informational texts. I make these vocabulary "tools" a priority in my lessons with middle school and high school students so they will be prepared to achieve their educational and personal goals.

As you use this textbook in your classroom, you will probably notice that it is quite different from other textbooks that you have used before. Instead of quietly writing sentences in your notebook with your head down during class, your teacher will lead you through dynamic, engaging activities that require you to share your ideas with the class and with a partner. I want to make sure that you can use these critical words appropriately and that you enjoy the process of creating and collaborating with classmates.

When you use this interactive curricula in class, it's important that you listen carefully to your teacher. Your teacher will ask you to follow many directions, such as repeating a word or sentence or providing an answer for an activity. You will also have to listen carefully to your classmates and partners—together, you will brainstorm interesting, appropriate answers for different activities.

As the school year continues, you will find yourself using these advanced academic words more and more in class. You will participate regularly in class discussions and become more comfortable using academic language. In essence, you will find yourself becoming a scholar of the English language—and having fun at it, too!

You can do it!

My very best regards,

Dr. Kate

Kate Kinsella, Ed.D., is a teacher educator at San Francisco State University and a highly sought after speaker and consultant to school districts throughout the United States regarding development of academic language and literacy across the K–12 subject areas. Her 25-year teaching career focus has been equipping children from diverse backgrounds with the communication, reading, and writing skills to be career and college ready. Dr. Kinsella remains active in K–12 classrooms by providing in-class coaching and by teaching an academic literacy class for adolescent English learners. Her extensive publishing career includes articles, chapters, English learners' dictionaries, and reading intervention programs. A former Fulbright TESOL lecturer, Dr. Kinsella was co-editor of the *CATESOL Journal* from 2000–2005 and served on the editorial board of the TESOL Journal from 1999–2003. Dr. Kinsella lives in California with her family, including two young adopted children, Jane Dzung from Vietnam and John Carlos from Guatemala.

Table of Contents

Grammar Lessons

acquire
verb

Say it: ac • **quire**   **Write it:** _____

Meaning	Example
to get or buy something	Andre has **acquired** many new CDs for his _____ .
Synonyms: obtain, accumulate	

Forms		Family
Present:		• **Noun:** acquisition
I/You/We/They	acquire	• **Adjective:** acquired
He/She/It	acquires	
Past:	acquired	

Word Partners

- _____ skills — Taking classes can help you **acquire new skills**.
- _____ information — The Internet makes it easy to **acquire information**.
- _____ knowledge — Reading is a great way to **acquire knowledge**.

Verbal Practice

Talk about It **Read** each sentence and **think** about how you would complete it.

Discuss your idea with your partner using the sentence frame.

Listen carefully to your partner's and classmates' ideas.

Write your favorite idea in the blank.

1. I recently **acquired** a new _____ .

2. A good way to **acquire** knowledge about other cultures is to _____ .

Writing Practice

Collaborate   **Work with your partner** to complete the sentence using the correct form of **acquire** and appropriate content.

To _____ a new skill, such as _____ , a person needs to

_____ every day.

Your Turn   **Work independently** to complete the sentence using the correct form of **acquire** and appropriate content.

In the last few years, I have _____ a collection of _____ .

Be an Academic Author   **Work independently** to write two sentences. In your first sentence, use **acquire** in the *simple past tense*. In your second sentence, use **acquire** in the *present perfect tense* and include a word partner.

❶ _____

_____

❷ _____

_____

> ### grammar tip
>
> The present perfect tense is formed with *has/have* + the past participle form of the verb. To make the past participle of regular verbs, add *–ed* or *–d*.
>
> She **has** acquir**ed** a new car.
>
> We **have** work**ed** here for two years.

Write an Academic Paragraph   **Complete** the paragraph using the correct form of **acquire** and original content.

It's much easier to _____ bad habits than it
❶

is to get rid of them. Even so, if you have _____ any bad habits over
❷

the years, you can change them if you put your mind to it. Choose just one bad habit, and

make a resolution to turn it into a _____ habit over the course of a
❸

month. For example, maybe you drink two cans or bottles of _____
❹

every day, even though all the sugar is not good for you. Start by cutting back to just one

_____ a day and replacing the other with water or natural juice. Do
❺

this for a couple of weeks and then _____ to drinking only water. After
❻

a few weeks, you can _____ some new good habits to replace your
❼

old bad habits.

adapt
verb

▶ **Say it:** a • **dapt** **Write it:** _____

Meaning	Example
to change to fit a new situation **Synonyms:** adjust, modify	Rats live all over the _____ because they **adapt** to many climates and _____ .

Forms	Family
Present: I/You/We/They adapt He/She/It adapts **Past:** adapted	• **Noun:** adaptation • **Adjective:** adaptable, adapted

Word Partners	
• _____ easily	While it can be difficult for older cats, most kittens **adapt easily** to a new home.
• _____ to change	Animals that do not **adapt to change** will die out.

Verbal Practice

Talk about It **Read** each sentence and **think** about how you would complete it.

Discuss your idea with your partner using the sentence frame.

Listen carefully to your partner's and classmates' ideas.

Write your favorite idea in the blank.

❶ If your parents move, you must **adapt** to a new _____ .

❷ During the Ice Ages, _____ **adapted** to changes in the environment.

Writing Practice

Collaborate **Work with your partner** to complete the sentence using the correct form of **adapt** and appropriate content.

All of the players on the team _____ easily to the new coach's

_____ .

Your Turn **Work independently** to complete the sentence using the correct form of **adapt** and appropriate content.

When Lana needed a costume for _____ , she took a white sheet and quickly

_____ it to be a _____ .

Be an Academic Author **Work independently** to write two sentences. In your first sentence, use **adapt** with a word partner. In your second sentence, use **adapt** with the modal verb *must*.

❶ _____

_____

❷ _____

_____

> ### grammar tip
>
> **Modal verbs are helping verbs that give additional meaning to the main verb.** *Must* **expresses necessity.**
>
> Animals **must adapt** to survive.
>
> I **must study** for my test tomorrow.

Write an Academic Paragraph **Complete** the paragraph using the correct form of **adapt** and original content.

Humans live in the world's driest deserts as well as in its wettest _____ .
❶

They live in deep valleys and near the tops of _____ . Some hardy
❷

_____ even live in Antarctica. Humans are able to live under many
❸

different conditions because they can _____ to their surroundings.
❹

In places where it is very cold, humans can _____ . When it gets too
❺

hot, they can go for a swim. Humans also build _____ to protect
❻

themselves from heat, cold, and rain. Humans _____ to and change their
❼

environment in order to _____ .
❽

adjust
verb

Academic Vocabulary Toolkit

Meanings	Examples
1. to get used to a situation *Synonym:* adapt	1. Mei **adjusted** _____ when she transferred to a new _____ .
2. to change something a little bit in order to make it better *Synonyms:* fix, correct	2. Tom **adjusted** the _____ on his phone so it wouldn't _____ anyone.

Forms	Family
Present: I/You/We/They adjust He/She/It adjusts *Past:* adjusted	• *Noun:* adjustment • *Adjective:* adjustable

Word Partners

- ____ (my/your/his/her/their/our) expectations

  I wanted a new phone for my birthday, but my mother lost her job so I have **adjusted my expectations**.

- ____ accordingly

  Consider how active you are and **adjust** your diet **accordingly**.

Verbal Practice

Talk about It   **Read** each sentence and **think** about how you would complete it.

Discuss your idea with your partner using the sentence frame.

Listen carefully to your partner's and classmates' ideas.

Write your favorite idea in the blank.

❶ I am slowly **adjusting** to _____ .

❷ We **adjusted** our expectations after the team _____ its first three games.

❸ You can **adjust** the settings of your _____ .

❹ When I walk with my _____ , I **adjust** my speed accordingly.

Writing Practice

Collaborate **Work with your partner** to complete the sentences using the correct form of **adjust** and appropriate content.

❶ When Carlos broke his _____ , he had to _____ to

_____ .

❷ It was too _____ in the room, so I _____ the

_____ .

Your Turn **Work independently** to complete the sentences using the correct form of **adjust** and appropriate content.

❶ I am finally _____ to the idea that _____ .

❷ The bride _____ her _____ before she walked down the aisle.

Be an Academic Author **Work independently** to write two sentences. In your first sentence, use **adjust** in the *present progressive tense* and include a word partner. In your second sentence, use **adjust** in the *simple past tense*.

MEANING ❶ _____

_____

MEANING ❷ _____

_____

> ### grammar tip
>
> The present progressive tense is formed with *am/is/are* + a verb ending in *–ing*.
>
> I **am adjusting** to my new neighborhood.
>
> She **is running** down the street.

Write an Academic Paragraph **Complete** the paragraph using the correct form of **adjust** and original content.

Not everything in life turns out how you want. It's important to be

able to _____ your expectations to avoid feeling frustrated every
          ❶

time something goes _____ . If you go on vacation and expect the
                    ❷

_____ to be always sunny, your family to be in a good mood all the
❸

time, and all of your activities to go exactly as you _____ them, your
                                                      ❹

expectations are _____ . Some things are going to go wrong. It might
                 ❺

rain. Your sister might complain about everything. If you _____ the
                                                          ❻

situation with realistic expectations, you will be able to _____ to
                                                           ❼

whatever situation comes your way.

affect
verb

▶ **Say it:** af • **fect**   **Write it:** _____

Meaning	Example
to influence or cause a change **Synonyms:** influence, impact, change	The _____ **affected** all the houses on our _____ .

Forms		Family
Present: I/You/We/They affect He/She/It affects **Past:** affected		• **Adjective:** affecting

Word Partners

- adversely _____   Cold weather **adversely affects** plant growth.
- _____ behavior   Some drugs **affect** people's **behavior**.
- directly _____   The price of gas **directly affects** how much people drive.

Verbal Practice

Talk about It   **Read** each sentence and **think** about how you would complete it.

Discuss your idea with your partner using the sentence frame.

Listen carefully to your partner's and classmates' ideas.

Write your favorite idea in the blank.

❶ Issues such as _____ directly **affect** our community.

❷ _____ can adversely **affect** your health.

8

Writing Practice

Collaborate **Work with your partner** to complete the sentence using the correct form of **affect** and appropriate content.

Staying up late to _____ might _____ your ability to pay attention in class the next day.

Your Turn **Work independently** to complete the sentence using the correct form of **affect** and appropriate content.

Do you agree that television adversely _____ the behavior of

_____ ?

Be an Academic Author **Work independently** to write two sentences. In your first sentence, use **affect** with the modal verb *might*. In your second sentence, use **affect** in the *simple present tense* and include a word partner.

❶ _____

_____

❷ _____

_____

> ## grammar tip
> In the simple present tense, the third person (*he, she, it*) form takes an –s or –es ending.
>
> Noise affects my concentration.
>
> Mr. Tom teaches my biology class.

Write an Academic Paragraph **Complete** the paragraph using the correct form of **affect** and original content.

Did you know that certain chemicals in food can directly

_____ your mood? For example, a chemical called serotonin helps
❶

regulate your _____ and feelings. Tryptophan, an amino acid found
❷

in protein-rich _____ like turkey, produces serotonin. You can
❸

also _____ your tryptophan levels by eating carbohydrates—but
❹

be careful! Refined carbohydrates such as sugar and white flour can adversely

_____ your mood by dramatically increasing blood sugar levels
❺

and _____ a "sugar crash." Complex carbohydrates like whole
❻

grains and _____ are better choices.
❼

alter
verb

▶ *Say it:* **al** • ter   *Write it:* _____

Meaning	Example
to make changes *Synonyms:* change, modify	Anyone can use _____ programs to **alter** a _____ .

Forms	Family
Present: I/You/We/They alter He/She/It alters *Past:* altered	• *Noun:* alteration • *Adjective:* altered

Word Partners	
• _____ the course of	The events of September 11, 2001, **altered the course of** American politics and foreign relations.
• _____ (my/your/his/her/their/our) plans	When we saw that it was raining, we **altered our plans** to go to the beach.

Verbal Practice

Talk about It **Read** each sentence and **think** about how you would complete it.

Discuss your idea with your partner using the sentence frame.

Listen carefully to your partner's and classmates' ideas.

Write your favorite idea in the blank.

❶ Lucia got into trouble when she **altered** her _____ .

❷ If it would be easier for you, I could **alter** my plans for _____ .

Writing Practice

Collaborate **Work with your partner** to complete the sentence using the correct form of **alter** and appropriate content.

In many science fiction movies, people _____ back in time and do things that

_____ the course of _____ .

Your Turn **Work independently** to complete the sentence using the correct form of **alter** and appropriate content.

Someday, scientists may invent a _____ that will completely

_____ the way we _____ .

Be an Academic Author **Work independently** to write two sentences. In your first sentence, use **alter** with the modal verb *could* and include a word partner. In your second sentence, use **alter** in the *simple past tense*.

❶ _____

_____

❷ _____

_____

> ## grammar tip
>
> **Modal verbs are helping verbs that give additional meaning to the main verb. *Could* expresses possibility.**
>
> Bad weather **could alter** our plans.
>
> This **could end** badly.

Write an Academic Paragraph **Complete** the paragraph using the correct form of **alter** and original content.

Online shopping has truly _____ the consumer experience.
❶

Today you can _____ virtually anything on the Internet with
❷

just one click. Online shopping has _____ both consumers
❸

and businesses. For example, small stores that sell special interest items like crafts or

_____ are able to reach more people online than with a physical store.
❹

In addition, individuals with full-time jobs can _____ goods that they
❺

make in their spare time for extra income. You can even sell some of your old possessions

on Web sites like _____ to earn extra money! Online shopping has
❻

_____ people's spending habits by giving them greater access to
❼

products and services.

alternative
noun

▶ **Say it:** al • **ter** • na • tive   *Write it:* _____

Meaning	Example
a choice, solution, or plan of action that is different from another	Walking to the _____ takes too long, and the bus only comes _____ an hour; so the best **alternative** is to ride a bike.

Forms	Family
• *Singular:* alternative • *Plural:* alternatives	• *Verb:* alternate • *Adjective:* alternative, alternate • *Adverb:* alternatively

Word Partners

• best _____	If you won't eat vegetables, fruit may be the **best alternative**.
• offer an _____	You should **offer an alternative** for people who don't eat fish.
• only _____	We don't want to wait at the side of the highway until a tow truck comes for our car, but it's the **only alternative**.

Verbal Practice

Talk about It   **Read** each sentence and **think** about how you would complete it.

Discuss your idea with your partner using the sentence frame.

Listen carefully to your partner's and classmates' ideas.

Write your favorite idea in the blank.

❶ If you don't like cereal for breakfast, then try _____ as an **alternative**.

❷ When it comes to choosing _____ , students at our school have numerous **alternatives**.

Writing Practice

Collaborate **Work with your partner** to complete the sentence using the correct form of **alternative** and appropriate content.

Studying for a test can be difficult, but the only _____ is to

_____ .

Your Turn **Work independently** to complete the sentence using the correct form of **alternative** and appropriate content.

Cars that run on _____ offer an _____ to cars that run on

_____ .

Be an Academic Author **Work independently** to write two sentences. In your first sentence, use **alternative** in the *singular form* and include a word partner. In your second sentence, use **alternative** in the *plural form* with the quantifier *numerous*.

❶ _____

_____

❷ _____

_____

grammar tip

Quantifiers are words that tell us how much or how many of something there is. They usually come before the noun they are describing.

In a city, there are **numerous** alternatives to driving.

I have **several** coins in my pocket.

Write an Academic Paragraph **Complete** the paragraph using the correct form of **alternative** and original content.

Finding a high-paying job with only a high school degree is no longer an

_____ . Some type of higher education is _____
❶   ❷

in today's economy. However, not everyone _____ to get a bachelor's
❸

degree. Two-year associate's _____ and certificate programs can
❹

prepare students for a wide range of _____ , such as fashion designer,
❺

chef, auto _____ , or computer specialist. Alternatively, students can
❻

start at a two-year college and later transfer to a four-year _____ . You
❼

always have the _____ of improving yourself and continuing your
❽

education.

approximately
adverb

Academic Vocabulary Toolkit

Meaning	Example	
close but not exactly **Synonyms:** about, around	Our plane _____ **approximately** _____ minutes late.	

Family

- **Noun:** approximation
- **Adjective:** approximate
- **Verb:** approximate

Word Partners

- _____ the same as

We were disappointed to find out that the gas mileage of our new car is **approximately the same as** that of our old car.

Verbal Practice

Talk about It **Read** each sentence and **think** about how you would complete it.

Discuss your idea with your partner using the sentence frame.

Listen carefully to your partner's and classmates' ideas.

Write your favorite idea in the blank.

❶ I wake up at **approximately** _____ on Saturday mornings.

❷ I spend **approximately** _____ hours watching TV every week.

Writing Practice

Collaborate   **Work with your partner** to complete the sentence using **approximately** and appropriate content.

There are _____ _____ students in our school.

Your Turn   **Work independently** to complete the sentence using **approximately** and appropriate content.

It takes me _____ the same amount of time to _____

as it does for me to _____ .

Be an Academic Author   **Work independently** to write two sentences. In your first sentence, use **approximately** with a verb in the *simple past tense*. In your second sentence, use **approximately** with a verb in the *simple present tense* and include the word partner *approximately the same as*.

❶ _____

_____

❷ _____

_____

> ### grammar tip
>
> **Adverbs usually go after the main verb.**
>
> The bus **stops <u>approximately</u>** ten times before it gets to my house.
>
> She **dances <u>beautifully</u>**.

Write an Academic Paragraph   **Complete** the paragraph using **approximately** and original content.

Did you know that _____ seventy percent of adults in the United
                    ❶

States are overweight or obese? Most people can avoid becoming obese by following

some healthy living _____ . First of all, avoid fast food, fried foods,
                      ❷

and _____ that are high in sugar, salt, and fat. Try to cut out soda,
       ❸

and instead drink _____ six to eight glasses of water a day. Be sure
          ❹

to eat plenty of fresh fruits and _____ . Most important, reduce your
            ❺

portion sizes! It's also important to be physically _____ . Aim to get
              ❻

_____ 60 minutes of exercise per day. This could be walking, running,
   ❼

biking, rollerblading, playing soccer, or playing _____—whatever you
              ❽

enjoy doing.

aspect
noun

Academic Vocabulary Toolkit

Meaning	Example
one part or one side of something	Mr. Barnes thinks _____ is one of the most important **aspects** of a good _____ .

Forms

- *Singular:* aspect
- *Plural:* aspects

Word Partners

• every _____	We analyzed **every aspect** of the problem before coming up with a solution.
• most important _____	Exploration and experimentation are the **most important aspects** of science.
• particular _____	There are **particular aspects** of the film that I did not like, but overall I thought it was well done.

Verbal Practice

Talk about It **Read** each sentence and **think** about how you would complete it.

Discuss your idea with your partner using the sentence frame.

Listen carefully to your partner's and classmates' ideas.

Write your favorite idea in the blank.

❶ There are many different **aspects** to my personality—for example, I am _____ but also _____ .

❷ One particular **aspect** of school that I like is _____ .

Writing Practice

Collaborate **Work with your partner** to complete the sentence using the correct form of **aspect** and appropriate content.

Before the game, the coach spent hours studying every _____ of the other

team's _____ .

Your Turn **Work independently** to complete the sentence using the correct form of **aspect** and appropriate content.

I think the most important _____ of music is _____ , but other

people think it is _____ .

Be an Academic Author **Work independently** to write two sentences. In your first sentence, use **aspect** in the *singular form*. In your second sentence, use **aspect** in the *plural form* and include a word partner.

❶ _____

_____

❷ _____

_____

> ### grammar tip
>
> Count nouns name things that can be counted. Count nouns have two forms, singular and plural. To make most count nouns plural, add –*s*.
>
> Look at all aspect**s** of the problem.
>
> He likes board game**s**.

Write an Academic Paragraph **Complete** the paragraph using the correct form of **aspect** and original content.

Do you prefer life in the city, the country, or someplace in between? Of course, there

are good and bad _____ to any place. In a city, there are lots of
                            ❶

things to do. However, cities are loud and _____ . In the country,
                                              ❷

on the other hand, _____ is peaceful and beautiful. There are
                        ❸

plenty of outdoor activities, such as boating and _____ . However,
                                                      ❹

if you don't have a _____ , it's hard to get around. To solve the
                        ❺

question of city or _____ life, people often turn to the suburbs.
                        ❻

In the _____ , you can often find some of the best—and worst—
            ❼

_____ of city and country living in one place.
            ❽

attain
verb

▶ **Say it:** at • **tain**　　　　**Write it:** _____

Meaning	Example
to achieve or gain something after making an effort *Synonym:* get	After waiting three years, Roberto finally **attained** U.S. _____ .

Forms	Family
Present: I/You/We/They　　attain He/She/It　　attains *Past:*　　attained	• *Adjective:* attainable

Word Partners	
• _____ a goal	In just four more years, I will **attain my goal** of graduating high school.
• _____ success	Mark Zuckerberg **attained** enormous **success** after creating Facebook.

Verbal Practice

Talk about It　**Read** each sentence and **think** about how you would complete it.

Discuss your idea with your partner using the sentence frame.

Listen carefully to your partner's and classmates' ideas.

Write your favorite idea in the blank.

❶ Someday I hope to **attain** my goal of _____ .

❷ You can **attain** success if you _____ .

Writing Practice

Collaborate   **Work with your partner** to complete the sentence using the correct form of **attain** and appropriate content.

_____ , an actor I admire, _____ great success with

_____ .

Your Turn   **Work independently** to complete the sentence using the correct form of **attain** and appropriate content.

One thing I hope to _____ in the next _____ years is a

_____ .

Be an Academic Author   **Work independently** to write two sentences. In your first sentence, use **attain** in the *simple past tense*. In your second sentence, use **attain** with the modal verb *can* and include a word partner.

❶ _____

_____

❷ _____

_____

> ### grammar tip
> Modal verbs are helping verbs that give additional meaning to the main verb. *Can* expresses ability.
>
> She <u>**can**</u> **attain** better grades.
>
> I <u>**can**</u> **help** you later.

Write an Academic Paragraph   **Complete** the paragraph using the correct form of **attain** and original content.

Greek mythology tells many tales of heroes who _____

❶

immortality. Heracles, one of the great heroes of Greek mythology, was the son of the

god Zeus and the mortal woman Alcmene. Zeus's _____ , the

❷

goddess Hera, hated Heracles. When Heracles was just a baby, Hera sent snakes into his

_____ . To her _____ , the baby Heracles

❸   **❹**

killed the snakes with his bare hands. When he _____ maturity,

❺

Heracles married Megara. Hera, still wildly _____ , drove Heracles to

❻

such madness that he killed his family. When Heracles _____ what

❼

he had done, he was _____ . As a punishment, Heracles undertook

❽

twelve difficult tasks. Once he completed his labors, Heracles, Greece's greatest hero, became

immortal.

bias
noun

Write it: _____

Meaning	Example
an opinion about someone or something that is not always fair or based on facts **Synonym:** prejudice	When it comes to dating, Lori has a _____ **bias** toward _____ guys.

Forms	Family
• **Singular:** bias • **Plural:** biases	• **Verb:** bias • **Adjective:** biased

Word Partners	
• gender _____	Words such as *policeman* and *fireman* are examples of **gender bias**.
• racial _____	That store is guilty of **racial bias**; it has no non-white workers.
• avoid _____	You can **avoid bias** in your writing by saying *firefighter* instead of *fireman*.

Verbal Practice

Talk about It **Read** each sentence and **think** about how you would complete it.

Discuss your idea with your partner using the sentence frame.

Listen carefully to your partner's and classmates' ideas.

Write your favorite idea in the blank.

❶ I have a **bias** in favor of people who _____ .

❷ Judges must avoid **biases** based on _____ or

_____ .

Writing Practice

Collaborate **Work with your partner** to complete the sentence using the correct form of **bias** and appropriate content.

I often come across examples of gender _____ when I _____ .

Your Turn **Work independently** to complete the sentence frames using the correct form of **bias** and appropriate content.

Some people think racial _____ is a thing of the past because

_____ .

Be an Academic Author **Work independently** to write two sentences. In your first sentence, use **bias** in the *singular form* and use a word partner. In your second sentence, use **bias** in the *plural form*.

❶ _____

_____

❷ _____

_____

> ### grammar tip
> Count nouns name things that can be counted. Count nouns have two forms, singular and plural. To make nouns that end in *s*, *ch*, or *x* plural, add –*es*.
>
> bias**es**, porch**es**, box**es**

Write an Academic Paragraph **Complete** the paragraph using the correct form of **bias** and original content.

The media includes newspapers, magazines, radio, _____ ❶ ,

and other means of communication that reach a large number of people. People

often accuse the _____ ❷ of bias. Some people think the

media has a _____ ❸ against conservatives; others think it

has a bias _____ ❹ liberals. However, if you pay attention

to the _____ ❺ , you may soon discover that the real

_____ ❻ of the media in the United States is in favor of conflict. To

sell advertising, the media want to keep you watching, _____ ❼ ,

or listening. They focus on conflict because it is more exciting than peace and

_____ ❽ .

biased
adjective

▶ **Say it:** bi · ased

Write it: _____

Meaning	Example	
unfairly favoring one thing, idea, person, or group over others **Synonyms:** prejudiced, influenced **Antonym:** unbiased	I think Diego is one of the _____ kids at his school, but I'm his _____ , so I could be **biased**!	

Family

- **Noun:** bias
- **Verb:** bias

Word Partners

• _____ against	Some female employees who were never promoted are accusing the company of being **biased against** women.
• _____ toward	People from Nashville tend to be **biased toward** country music.
• _____ in favor of	I think my parents are **biased in favor of** my brother.

Verbal Practice

Talk about It **Read** each sentence and **think** about how you would complete it.

Discuss your idea with your partner using the sentence frame.

Listen carefully to your partner's and classmates' ideas.

Write your favorite idea in the blank.

❶ When I'm choosing a book to read, I'm **biased** toward _____ .

❷ I think that many people in this country are **biased** against

_____ .

Writing Practice

Collaborate **Work with your partner** to complete the sentence using **biased** and appropriate content.

What happened at the _____ was unfair because the _____

was completely _____ in favor of _____ .

Your Turn **Work independently** to complete the sentence using **biased** and appropriate content.

The town's Web site will give you a _____ account of life there; for a more

accurate picture, you should _____ .

Be an Academic Author **Work independently** to write two sentences. In your first sentence, use **biased** with the word partner *against*. In your second sentence, use **biased** with the word partner *in favor of*.

❶ _____

_____

❷ _____

_____

> **grammar tip**
>
> **An adjective usually comes before the noun it describes.**
>
> a **biased** account
>
> a **big** house
>
> a **green** jacket

Write an Academic Paragraph **Complete** the paragraph using **biased** and original content.

Studies show that some parents in India are _____ toward sons
❶

and _____ daughters. Traditionally, when a couple in India
❷

marries, the bride's family pays the wedding expenses and a dowry, or bride price, to the

_____ family. This means a lot of financial strain for a family with
❸

several _____ and a lot of financial gain for a family with several
❹

_____ . Furthermore, sons stay with their parents, while a girl moves in
❺

with her _____ and his family. Parents prefer to have a child who will
❻

take care of them when they are old rather than one that will _____
❼

them. The Indian government is taking action to change this _____
❽

situation, but it is a slow process to change old traditions.

capable
adjective

Say it: ca • pa • ble   **Write it:** _____

Meaning	Example
having the ability to do something well	**Capable** EMTs _____ think and act quickly to _____ people's lives.
Synonyms: competent, able	
Antonym: incapable	

Family

Noun: capability
Adverb: capably

Word Partners

- perfectly _____   I am **perfectly capable** of changing a tire; I just don't want to.
- in _____ hands   With the new coach, our track team is now **in capable hands**.

Verbal Practice

Talk about It   **Read** each sentence and **think** about how you would complete it.

Discuss your idea with your partner using the sentence frame.

Listen carefully to your partner's and classmates' ideas.

Write your favorite idea in the blank.

❶ I am perfectly **capable** of _____ even though I rarely do.

❷ A **capable** musician should be able to _____ .

24

Writing Practice

Collaborate **Work with your partner** to complete the sentence using **capable** and appropriate content.

Our teacher would be very comfortable leaving our class in the _____ hands

of _____ .

Your Turn **Work independently** to complete the sentence frame using **capable** and appropriate content.

Cell phones are now _____ of performing many functions, such as

_____ and _____ .

Be an Academic Author **Work independently** to write two sentences. In your first sentence, use **capable** with a *singular noun*. In your second sentence, use **capable** with a *plural noun*. Include a word partner in one sentence.

❶ _____

_____

❷ _____

_____

> ### grammar tip
> **An adjective usually comes before the nouns it describes.**
> a <u>capable</u> professional
> a <u>big</u> house
> a <u>green</u> jacket

Write an Academic Paragraph **Complete** the paragraph using **capable** and original content.

Inside each of us there is a superhero waiting to come out and do things we never believed

we were _____①_____ of. There have been many documented incidents

of ordinary _____②_____ lifting cars, fighting bears, and performing other

amazing feats of courage and strength when their _____③_____ were in

danger. Fear or stress _____④_____ our bodies to produce adrenaline,

which makes us physically ready to face danger. Adrenaline causes our heart rate to

_____⑤_____ and our muscles to contract. Our bodies then become more

efficient at converting glycogen into glucose, which _____⑥_____ energy to

our muscles. We become temporarily stronger, faster, and _____⑦_____ of

much more than we usually are.

circumstance
noun

▶ **Say it:** **cir** • cum • stance   **Write it:** _____

Meaning	Example
a condition that affects a situation	I wonder what **circumstances** caused the _____ to abandon their _____ .

Forms	Family
• **Singular:** circumstance • **Plural:** circumstances	**Adjective:** circumstantial **Adverb:** circumstantially

Word Partners	
• certain _____ s	In **certain circumstances**, such as illness, it is possible for a student to make up an exam.
• _____ surrounding	The **circumstances surrounding** the man's death were mysterious.
• under the _____ s	Our star quarterback is injured; **under the circumstances**, we were very happy just to have won.

Verbal Practice

Talk about It **Read** each sentence and **think** about how you would complete it.

Discuss your idea with your partner using the sentence frame.

Listen carefully to your partner's and classmates' ideas.

Write your favorite idea in the blank.

❶ In certain **circumstances**, it might be acceptable for a person to

_____ .

❷ In history class, we had to explain the **circumstances** surrounding

_____ .

Writing Practice

Collaborate   **Work with your partner** to complete the sentence using the correct form of **circumstance** and appropriate content.

I told my teacher that I couldn't _____ because of a special

_____ .

Your Turn   **Work independently** to complete the sentence using the correct form of **circumstance** and appropriate content.

It's _____ outside today, so under the _____ we can't

_____ .

Be an Academic Author   **Work independently** to write two sentences. In your first sentence, use **circumstance** in the *singular form*. In your second sentence, use **circumstance** in the *plural form* and include a word partner.

❶ _____

_____

❷ _____

_____

> ### grammar tip
> Count nouns name things that can be counted. Count nouns have two forms, singular and plural. To make most count nouns plural, add *–s.*
>
> Circumstance**s** forced me to change my plan**s**.

Write an Academic Paragraph   **Complete** the paragraph using the correct form of **circumstance** and original content.

Almost 3,500 years ago, the Egyptian pharaoh known as King Tut died at the age of

18 under mysterious _____ . A hole in the back of his mummy's
      ❶

skull led many Egyptologists to _____ that he may have been
      ❷

_____ . However, using new technology and DNA testing,
     ❸

scientists have arrived at a different _____ . King Tut apparently
      ❹

suffered from a bone disorder that left him unable to walk normally. His death was likely

_____ by a combination of his bone disease, a leg injury, and
     ❺

the malaria virus. The hole in his skull probably _____ during the
        ❻

mummification process. Thanks to technological advances, the _____
         ❼

surrounding King Tut's death are now less of a mystery.

claim
verb

Academic Vocabulary Toolkit

Meanings	Examples
1. to ask for or take something that is yours	1. After the flight, we **claimed** our _____ .
2. to say that something is true but not have proof *Synonym:* assert	2. In his essay, Tyler **claimed** electric cars were _____ , but he had no _____ to support his idea.

Forms

Present:
I/You/We/They　　claim
He/She/It　　claims

Past:　　claimed

Family

• *Noun:* claim

Word Partners

• ____ credit for	You shouldn't **claim credit for** something you didn't write.
• ____ responsibility for	John **claimed responsibility for** the prank.

Verbal Practice

Talk about It **Read** each sentence and **think** about how you would complete it.

Discuss your idea with your partner using the sentence frame.

Listen carefully to your partner's and classmates' ideas.

Write your favorite idea in the blank.

❶ If you lose something at the _____ , you can sometimes **claim** it at the lost and found.

❷ If you win _____ , you must go onstage to **claim** your prize.

❸ I once **claimed** to be sick, just so I could _____ .

❹ A group of students **claimed** responsibility for _____ .

Writing Practice

Collaborate **Work with your partner** to complete the sentences using the correct form of **claim** and appropriate content.

❶ Explorers came to America and _____ land for _____ .

❷ Many people _____ to have seen _____ , but their stories have never been proven.

Your Turn **Work independently** to complete the sentences using the correct form of **claim** and appropriate content.

❶ If the police find your stolen _____ , you should be able to go to the police station and _____ it.

❷ The politician _____ credit for the _____ , but he really had nothing to do with it.

Be an Academic Author **Work independently** to write two sentences. In your first sentence, use **claim** in the *simple past tense*. In your second sentence, use **claim** in the *simple present tense* and include a word partner.

MEANING ❶ _____

_____

MEANING ❷ _____

_____

> ### grammar tip
>
> **To make the simple past tense of regular verbs, add *—ed* or *—d*.**
>
> She claim**ed** to be a princess.
>
> He love**d** all his children the same.

Write an Academic Paragraph **Complete** the paragraph using the correct form of **claim** and original content.

When the king of England died in 1066, a distant relative of the king named William, Duke of Norway, _____ ❶ the throne. William _____ ❷ that the king had promised the throne to him before he died. However, other men also came forward and _____ ❸ the throne as their own, including the king of Norway and Harold, the brother of the queen of England. First, Harold and his army _____ ❹ the king of Norway's troops and won. Then, William and Harold _____ ❺ to settle the claim by arranging a battle. However, in just six hours, William's army _____ ❻ Harold's. William then _____ ❼ the throne and became king of England.

clarify
verb

> **Say it:** **clar** • i • fy　　　　**Write it:** _____

Academic Vocabulary Toolkit

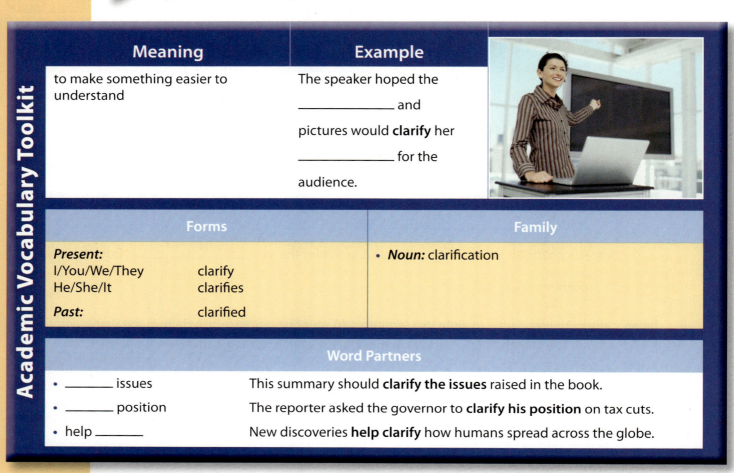

Meaning	Example
to make something easier to understand	The speaker hoped the _____ and pictures would **clarify** her _____ for the audience.

Forms	Family
Present: I/You/We/They　　clarify He/She/It　　clarifies **Past:**　　clarified	• **Noun:** clarification

Word Partners

• _____ issues	This summary should **clarify the issues** raised in the book.
• _____ position	The reporter asked the governor to **clarify his position** on tax cuts.
• help _____	New discoveries **help clarify** how humans spread across the globe.

Verbal Practice

Talk about It　**Read** each sentence and **think** about how you would complete it.

Discuss your idea with your partner using the sentence frame.

Listen carefully to your partner's and classmates' ideas.

Write your favorite idea in the blank.

❶ When you're explaining how to do something, you can **clarify** your instructions by

_____ .

❷ Flight attendants help **clarify** emergency procedures for passengers by

_____ .

Writing Practice

Collaborate **Work with your partner** to complete the sentence using the correct form of **clarify** and appropriate content.

The president _____ his position on _____ by

_____ .

Your Turn **Work independently** to complete the sentence using the correct form of **clarify** and appropriate content.

Our teacher has _____ the issues that we need to discuss in our

_____ .

Be an Academic Author **Work independently** to write two sentences. In your first sentence, use **clarify** in the *present perfect tense*. In your second sentence, use **clarify** in the *simple present tense* and include a word partner.

❶ _____

_____

❷ _____

_____

> **grammar tip**
>
> The present perfect tense is formed with *has/have* + the past participle form of the verb. To make the past participle of verbs that end in a consonant + *y*, change the *y* to *i*, and add −*ed*.
>
> She **has** clarified her ideas in writing.
>
> I **have** carried the bag upstairs.

Write an Academic Paragraph **Complete** the paragraph using the correct form of **clarify** and original content.

When teenagers get their first job, they are usually excited about

earning _____ ❶ . However, understanding what

is expected of you at a new job can be _____ ❷ . At a new babysitting

job, for example, you should _____ ❸ what you need to do if the baby

cries or if the toddler wants _____ ❹ . Sometimes people are afraid to

ask for clarification because they don't want to look _____ ❺ . However,

if you _____ ❻ your hours, responsibilities, and what you will be paid

beforehand, your employer will think you are _____ ❼ for taking initiative,

and it will make your work life much easier.

communicate
verb

Say it: com • **mu** • ni • cate   ***Write it:*** _____

Meaning	Example
to talk or write to someone	Letters were once a common way to **communicate** with _____ ; today, people can call or _____ .

Forms	Family
Present: I/You/We/They communicate He/She/It communicates **Past:** communicated	• **Noun:** communication • **Adjective:** communicative • **Adverb:** communicatively

Word Partners

• ability to _____	A successful leader has the **ability to communicate** his or her ideas.
• _____ effectively	If you are at a concert, speaking softly is not the best way to **communicate effectively** with others.

Verbal Practice

Talk about It   **Read** each sentence and **think** about how you would complete it.

Discuss your idea with your partner using the sentence frame.

Listen carefully to your partner's and classmates' ideas.

Write your favorite idea in the blank.

❶ Before Web sites such as _____ , people **communicated** with friends and family by calling and writing letters.

❷ Great songwriters have the ability to **communicate** their ideas using _____ .

Writing Practice

Collaborate   **Work with your partner** to complete the sentence using the correct form of **communicate** and appropriate content.

I usually _____ with my friends by _____ rather than by

_____ because it's _____ .

Your Turn   **Work independently** to complete the sentence using the correct form of **communicate** and appropriate content.

The best teachers _____ effectively using _____ and

_____ .

Be an Academic Author   **Work independently** to write two sentences. In your first sentence, use **communicate** in the *simple present tense* with a person's name. In your second sentence, use **communicate** in the *simple past tense* and include a word partner.

❶ _____

_____

❷ _____

_____

> ### grammar tip
>
> **In the simple present tense, the third person (*he/she/it*) form takes an *–s* or *–es* ending.**
>
> She communicate**s** using American Sign Language.
>
> He go**es** to the library after school.

Write an Academic Paragraph   **Complete** the paragraph using the correct form of **communicate** and original content.

From phone calls to text messages, humans _____ in a variety of
❶

ways. But have you ever realized how often people _____ with others
❷

without using words? There are two _____ of communication—verbal
❸

and nonverbal. Verbal communication involves _____ with someone
❹

by speaking aloud. Nonverbal communication is when you _____
❺

using visual clues. This often includes body language, such as nodding or

_____ . Humans _____ a significant amount of
❻   ❼

information using body language, including their feelings and moods.

communication
noun

▶ **Say it:** com • mu • ni • **ca** • tion **Write it:** _____

Meaning	Example
the act of talking or writing to someone	One _____ form of **communication** today is _____ .

Family

- **Noun:** communicator
- **Verb:** communicate
- **Adjective:** communicative

Word Partners

• lines of _____	The two countries keep their **lines of communication** open; the ambassadors are in contact with each other.
• means of _____	Texting is my usual **means of communication**.

Verbal Practice

Talk about It **Read** each sentence and **think** about how you would complete it.

Discuss your idea with your partner using the sentence frame.

Listen carefully to your partner's and classmates' ideas.

Write your favorite idea in the blank.

❶ Lines of **communication** often break down when people _____ .

❷ _____ is an effective means of **communication** for students.

Writing Practice

Collaborate   **Work with your partner** to complete the sentence using **communication** and appropriate content.

Long ago, _____ was a popular means of _____ .

Your Turn   **Work independently** to complete the sentence using **communication** and appropriate content.

One way to improve _____ between children and their parents would be

_____ .

Be an
Academic
Author

Work independently to write two sentences. In your first sentence, use **communication** with the word partner *means of communication*. In your second sentence, use **communication** with the word partner *lines of communication*.

❶ _____

_____

❷ _____

_____

Write an
Academic
Paragraph

Complete the paragraph using **communication** and original content.

All animals have their own form of _____ . Bears growl, dolphins

❶

trill, and birds _____ . While most animals, with the exception

❷

of _____ , can't speak human languages, they are still able to

❸

_____ their desires and needs in ways we can learn to understand. For

❹

example, when a dog wags its tail or a cat purrs, it is _____ that it is

❺

happy. When an animal _____ or hisses, it might be guarding its territory

❻

or offspring. Studies of animal _____ have shown that, even if animals

❼

don't talk as much as they do in the movies, they really do have something to say.

compatible
adjective

Academic Vocabulary Toolkit

Meaning	Example	
when two things get along or work well together **Antonym:** incompatible	Dogs and _____ are not usually **compatible** pets, but my dog and cat are great _____ .	

Family

- **Noun:** compatibility

Word Partners

• _____ with	The results of our science experiment were **compatible with** the results of the rest of the class.
• completely _____	I've had no problems using my new music-writing program; it's **completely compatible** with my computer.

Verbal Practice

Talk about It **Read** each sentence and **think** about how you would complete it.

Discuss your idea with your partner using the sentence frame.

Listen carefully to your partner's and classmates' ideas.

Write your favorite idea in the blank.

❶ Our dreams are not always completely **compatible** with _____ .

❷ Outgoing people are usually most **compatible** with people who like to _____ .

Writing Practice

Collaborate **Work with your partner** to complete the sentence using **compatible** and appropriate content.

_____ and _____ are two types of clothing

that are not _____ with each other.

Your Turn **Work independently** to complete the sentence using **compatible** and appropriate content.

Unfortunately, my _____ and I do not have _____

ideas about _____ .

Be an Academic Author **Work independently** to write two sentences. In your first sentence, use **compatible** with a *plural noun*. In your second sentence, use **compatible** with the word partner *completely compatible*.

❶ _____

_____

❷ _____

_____

> ### grammar tip
> Adjectives do not have plural forms. Do not add an *–s* to adjectives when they describe plural nouns.
> <u>compatible</u> ideas
> <u>loud</u> dogs
> <u>puffy</u> marshmallows

Write an Academic Paragraph **Complete** the paragraph using **compatible** and original content.

Compatibility is an important _____ in choosing a new computer.
                                              ❶

Make sure your new computer is _____ with any hardware you own,
                                              ❷

such as your keyboard and printer. In addition, any software, such as word processing programs

or games, must be _____ with your hardware in order to perform
                          ❸

smoothly. For example, if you have a library of video games, you should make sure that they

are _____ with your new computer's operating system. If they are
        ❹

incompatible, your software won't _____ well—or at all. If you need
                                              ❺

help, you can _____ computer specialists who can help you make sure
                      ❻

your new computer will be _____ with your software and hardware.
                                      ❼

complex
adjective

Say it: com • **plex**

Write it: _____

Meaning	Example
having many parts that are hard to understand **Synonyms:** intricate, involved	The human _____ is so **complex** we may never fully _____ it.

Family

- **Noun:** complexity
- **Adverb:** complexly

Word Partners

• _____ issue	Climate change is a **complex issue** with no quick or easy answers.
• _____ system	My history teacher has a very **complex system** for grading papers; she gives points for many different categories.

Verbal Practice

Talk about It   **Read** each sentence frame and **think** about how you would complete it.

Discuss your idea with your partner using the sentence frame.

Listen carefully to your partner's and classmates' ideas.

Write your favorite idea in the blank.

1. An ecosystem, a football team, and _____ are examples of **complex** systems.

2. As you begin taking more advanced science classes, the _____ become more **complex**.

Writing Practice

Collaborate **Work with your partner** to complete the sentence using **complex** and appropriate content.

Personal relationships can become _____ when two people

_____ .

Your Turn **Work independently** to complete the sentence using **complex** and appropriate content.

As an adult, I would like to work at solving _____ issues like

_____ and _____ .

Be an
Academic
Author

Work independently to write two sentences. In your first sentence, use **complex** with a *plural noun*. In your second sentence, use **complex** with the word partner *complex system*.

❶ _____

_____

❷ _____

_____

> ## grammar tip
>
> Adjectives do not have plural forms. Do not add an –*s* to adjectives when they describe plural nouns.
>
> <u>complex</u> issues
>
> <u>loud</u> dogs
>
> <u>puffy</u> marshmallows

Write an
Academic
Paragraph

Complete the paragraph using **complex** and original content.

Looking at the world as a series of _____ systems can help us
❶

understand our surroundings. A _____ has parts that are connected
❷

with each other. A system also has a function, or _____ . In a
❸

_____ system, the parts interact and produce a new behavior. It is
❹

impossible to predict the behavior of a complex _____ by looking at one
❺

part of it. For example, a bee hive is a _____ system, but you can't tell
❻

much about the bee hive by looking at a single _____ . Of course, you
❼

can learn a lot by studying one thing, like a bee, very closely. However, if you fail to consider how

that one part fits into a _____ , your understanding will be limited.
❽

compromise
verb

▶ *Say it:* **com** • pro • mise   *Write it:* _____

<table>
<tr><td colspan="2">Meaning</td><td>Example</td></tr>
</table>

Meaning	Example
to agree to something different than what you originally wanted	Bill doesn't like cats, and Sara doesn't like _____ , so they **compromised** and got a _____ instead.

Forms		Family
Present: I/You/We/They compromise He/She/It compromises *Past:* compromised		• *Noun:* compromise • *Adjective:* compromising

Word Partners

• need to _____	In any type of relationship, you will **need to compromise** with the other person about some things.
• willing to _____	When people are **willing to compromise**, it's easy to reach an agreement.

Verbal Practice

Talk about It   **Read** each sentence frame and **think** about how you would complete it.

Discuss your idea with your partner using the sentence frame.

Listen carefully to your partner's and classmates' ideas.

Write your favorite idea in the blank.

❶ When I go shopping, I need to **compromise** between what I can afford and

_____ .

❷ The students wanted to use their books in the final exam, so the teacher

compromised and let them use their _____ , but not

their textbooks.

Academic Vocabulary Toolkit

Writing Practice

Collaborate **Work with your partner** to complete the sentence using the correct form of **compromise** and appropriate content.

Louis wants to have pizza for dinner, but his brother Mario wants to eat Chinese food. They

should _____ and get _____ instead.

Your Turn **Work independently** to complete the sentence using the correct form of **compromise** and appropriate content.

I can't always afford what I want, but I never _____ when it comes to

_____ .

Be an **Work independently** to write two sentences. In your first sentence, use **compromise** in the
Academic *present tense* with the adverb of frequency *never*. In your second sentence, use **compromise** with
Author a word partner.

❶ _____

_____

❷ _____

_____

> ### grammar tip
> Adverbs of frequency are words that show how often something happens. They usually go before the main verb.
>
> She will **never compromise** her ideals.
>
> He **generally** doesn't eat fish.

Write an **Complete** the paragraph using the correct form of **compromise** and original
Academic content.
Paragraph

A willingness to _____ is an important part of a friendship. It shows that
❶

you care more about your _____ than you do about getting your own
❷

way. However, when you and a friend _____ , it can be difficult to find
❸

a compromise that works for you both. Compromising doesn't mean that you have to agree to

everything. Instead, consider what you are willing and unwilling to _____
❹

on. If your friend wants to do something dangerous, such as _____ ,
❺

you shouldn't go along with it. On the other hand, if it is something that you simply don't

like, such as _____ , you could give it a try. Your friend could also
❻

_____ by agreeing to do what you want the next time.
❼

conflict
verb

► **Say it:** con • **flict**   **Write it:** _____

<table>
<tr><th colspan="2">Meaning</th><th colspan="2">Example</th></tr>
<tr><td colspan="2">to differ</td><td colspan="2">When Greg and Emma's explanations **conflicted**, the _____ asked them both to meet in his _____ .</td></tr>
</table>

Academic Vocabulary Toolkit

Forms		Family
Present:		• **Noun:** conflict
I/You/We/They	conflict	• **Adjective:** conflicting, conflicted
He/She/It	conflicts	
Past:	conflicted	

Word Partners

- _____ with   The promise she made to you **conflicted with** the promise she made to me.
- _____ over   The neighbors **conflicted over** the remodeling plans for the apartment building.

Verbal Practice

Talk about It   **Read** each sentence frame and **think** about how you would complete it.

Discuss your idea with your partner using the sentence frame.

Listen carefully to your partner's and classmates' ideas.

Write your favorite idea in the blank.

❶ If you play a sport such as _____ , even when you **conflict** with the coach, you have to _____ .

❷ Teenagers and their parents often **conflict** over _____ .

Writing Practice

Collaborate **Work with your partner** to complete the sentence using the correct form of **conflict** and appropriate content.

Last summer, what I wanted to do _____ with what

_____ .

Your Turn **Work independently** to complete the sentence using the correct form of **conflict** and appropriate content.

When my beliefs have _____ with my friends' actions, I have usually

_____ .

Be an Academic Author **Work independently** to write two sentences. In your first sentence, use **conflict** in the *simple present tense*. In your second sentence, use **conflict** in the *present perfect tense* and include a word partner.

❶ _____

_____

❷ _____

_____

> ### grammar tip
>
> The present perfect tense is formed with *has/have* + the past participle form of the verb. To make the past participle of regular verbs, add *–ed* or *–d*.
>
> have conflict**ed**, has receiv**ed**, have wonder**ed**

Write an Academic Paragraph **Complete** the paragraph using the correct form of **conflict** and original content.

Being a teenager is not easy—but being a parent isn't easy, either. Even when parents and

children are close, they can still _____ over rules. This conflict is
                                        ❶

_____ because children and parents usually have different goals. For
        ❷

example, a parent's _____ is to keep his or her child safe, while a child's
                        ❸

job is to explore the world. As children grow, parents continue to try to keep their sons and

daughters safe while children continue to _____ boundaries. This concern
                                              ❹

for safety particularly _____ with a teenager's desire for more freedom.
                          ❺

Teenagers might know that their parents have their best _____ at heart;
                                                            ❻

but at the same time, they want to be treated like _____ .
                                                        ❼

consume
verb

Say it: con • **sume**   **Write it:** _____

Academic Vocabulary Toolkit

Meanings	Examples
1. to eat, drink, or buy something	**1.** The average _____ **consumes** _____ pounds of added sugar a year.
2. to use something up	**2.** _____ **consume** less fuel than _____ .

Forms

Verb Forms
Present:
I/You/We/They   consume
He/She/It   consumes
Past: consumed

Family

- **Noun:** consumption
- **Adjective:** consumable

Word Partners

- _____ less   Most Americans should **consume less** salt.
- _____ energy   Clothes dryers **consume energy**, but hanging up your clothes to dry doesn't.

Verbal Practice

Talk about It **Read** each sentence and **think** about how you would complete it.

Discuss your idea with your partner using the sentence.

Listen carefully to your partner's and classmates' ideas.

Write your favorite idea in the blank.

❶ I can easily **consume** a lot of _____ as a snack.

❷ Some people will **consume** only _____ when they are on a diet.

❸ What will we do after we have **consumed** all the _____ in the world?

❹ Homework and _____ are **consuming** most of my weekends.

Writing Practice

Collaborate   **Work with your partner** to complete the sentence using the correct form of **consume** and appropriate content.

Many students find that _____ is _____ most of

their time.

Your Turn   **Work independently** to complete the sentence using the correct form of **consume** and appropriate content.

In the future people will _____ less _____ in

their everyday lives.

**Be an
Academic
Author**   **Work independently** to write two sentences using Meaning 2. In your first sentence, use **consume** in the *present progressive tense*. In your second sentence, use **consume** with the modal verb *will* and include a word partner.

❶ _____

_____

❷ _____

_____

> ## grammar tip
>
> **The present progressive tense is formed with *am/is/are* + a verb ending in *–ing*.**
>
> Americans **are consuming** more chocolate.
>
> I **am running** down the street.

**Write an
Academic
Paragraph**   **Complete** the paragraph using the correct form of **consume** and original content.

Americans have a high rate of consumption, and this waste is hurting the

_____ . When something breaks, such as a _____ ,
       ❶   ❷

many consumers simply buy another instead of trying to fix it. Americans also

_____ a lot of pre-packaged food. For example, instead of
      ❸

buying a large box of _____ , shoppers often buy small, single-
                       ❹

serving bags, which use more _____ and are more expensive.
                                ❺

Unfortunately, creating and disposing of these products also _____
                                                                 ❻

a lot of resources. There is no simple solution, but we can try to reduce how much we

_____ , reuse materials, and recycle as much as we can.
      ❼

controversial
adjective

▶ **Say it:** con • tro • **ver** • sial   ***Write it:*** _____

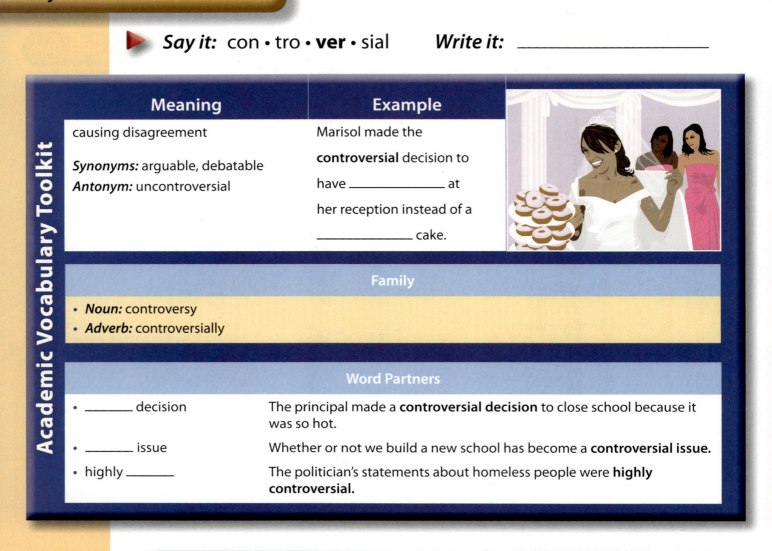

Academic Vocabulary Toolkit

Meaning	Example
causing disagreement **Synonyms:** arguable, debatable **Antonym:** uncontroversial	Marisol made the **controversial** decision to have _____ at her reception instead of a _____ cake.

Family

- **Noun:** controversy
- **Adverb:** controversially

Word Partners

• _____ decision	The principal made a **controversial decision** to close school because it was so hot.
• _____ issue	Whether or not we build a new school has become a **controversial issue.**
• highly _____	The politician's statements about homeless people were **highly controversial.**

Verbal Practice

Talk about It   **Read** each sentence and **think** about how you would complete it.

Discuss your idea with your partner using the sentence frame.

Listen carefully to your partner's and classmates' ideas.

Write your favorite idea in the blank.

1 Nowadays, _____ is a much less **controversial** issue than it was fifty years ago.

2 Politicians often try to avoid making **controversial** decisions because they

_____ .

Writing Practice

Collaborate **Work with your partner** to complete the sentence using **controversial** and appropriate content.

At some schools, the decision about _____ can become

highly _____ .

Your Turn **Work independently** to complete the sentence using **controversial** and appropriate content.

I sometimes try to avoid talking about _____ issues such as politics and

religion because _____ .

Be an **Work independently** to write two sentences. In your first sentence, use **controversial** with a *plural*
Academic *noun*. In your second sentence, use **controversial** with the word partner *controversial issue*.
Author

❶ _____

_____

❷ _____

_____

> **grammar tip**
>
> Adjectives do not have plural forms. Do not add an –*s* to adjectives when they describe plural nouns.
>
> <u>controversial</u> issues
>
> <u>loud</u> dogs
>
> <u>puffy</u> marshmallows

Write an **Complete** the paragraph using **controversial** and original content.
Academic
Paragraph
When most of us think of breakfast, we think of toast or _____ . For the
❶

Chicago School Board, however, breakfast has become a _____ issue.
❷

The school board realized that students have trouble _____ if they
❸

arrive at school hungry. To prevent this, Chicago schools started _____
❹

breakfast to students in their classrooms. What is so _____ about this?
❺

Unfortunately, some students have food allergies. If they touch, or sometimes even smell, the

_____ that they are allergic to, they could have a terrible reaction. Some
❻

parents are worried and want to see the program _____ . Who would
❼

have thought that breakfast could start a controversy?

cooperate
verb

Say it: co • **op** • er • ate   **Write it:** _____

<table>
<tr><th colspan="2">Meaning</th><th colspan="2">Example</th></tr>
<tr><td colspan="2">to work together toward the same goal</td><td colspan="2">Gloria wanted to go _____ , but her _____ refused to **cooperate.**</td></tr>
</table>

Forms		Family
Present: I/You/We/They cooperate He/She/It cooperates **Past:** cooperated		• **Noun:** cooperation • **Adjective:** cooperative • **Adverb:** cooperatively

Word Partners

• agree to _____	The two witnesses **agreed to cooperate** with the authorities to find the thief.
• refuse to _____	Children often **refuse to cooperate** with a new babysitter.

Verbal Practice

Talk about It   **Read** each sentence and **think** about how you would complete it.

Discuss your idea with your partner using the sentence frame.

Listen carefully to your partner's and classmates' ideas.

Write your favorite idea in the blank.

❶ The two nations are **cooperating** in an effort to

_____ .

❷ If a student refuses to **cooperate** in class, the teacher usually

_____ .

Writing Practice

Collaborate **Work with your partner** to complete the sentence using the correct form of **cooperate** and appropriate content.

In order to _____ , prehistoric people _____

with each other.

Your Turn **Work independently** to complete the sentence using the correct form of **cooperate** and appropriate content.

In the movie _____ , the main characters agree to _____

so that they can _____ .

Be an Academic Author **Work independently** to write two sentences. In your first sentence, use **cooperate** in the *simple past tense*. In your second sentence, use **cooperate** in the *present progressive tense*.

❶ _____

_____

❷ _____

_____

> ### grammar tip
>
> **The present progressive tense is formed with *am/is/are* + a verb ending in *–ing*.**
>
> I **am cooperating** with my sister to clean our room.
>
> They **are acting** in a play.

Write an Academic Paragraph **Complete** the paragraph using the correct form of **cooperate** and original content.

Many students today hope to go to college to study business. Their

_____ is to become a successful businessperson working for or
❶

perhaps owning a _____ . Aside from a college degree, what does it
❷

take to be a _____ businessperson? Successful businesspeople are
❸

competive and _____ . At the same time, however, they understand
❹

how important it is to _____ with others. Business is not done alone. It
❺

requires people to _____ with others to find solutions to problems. If
❻

you don't like the idea of brainstorming and _____ with other people,
❼

then business is probably not the field for you.

correspond
verb

▶ **Say it:** cor • re • **spond**   **Write it:** _____

Meanings	Examples
1. to write to someone	**1.** In the past, people **corresponded** by writing _____ .
2. to agree or match	**2.** The position of _____ in Great Britain **corresponds** to _____ in the United States.

Forms		Family
Present:		• **Noun:** correspondence, correspondent
I/You/We/They	correspond	• **Adjective:** corresponding
He/She/It	corresponds	• **Adverb:** correspondingly
Past:	corresponded	

Word Partners
• closely _____ to   The movie **closely corresponds to** the video game it is based on.

Verbal Practice

Talk about It **Read** each sentence and **think** about how you would complete it.

Discuss your idea with your partner using the sentence frame.

Listen carefully to your partner's and classmates' ideas.

Write your favorite idea in the blank.

❶ I don't **correspond** regularly with anyone, but I do write _____ .

❷ If I could **correspond** with someone from the past, I would be pen pals with

_____ .

❸ In the old grading system, an 85 **corresponded** to a letter grade of

_____ .

❹ I think the character _____ in the movie

_____ closely **corresponds** to my personality.

Writing Practice

Collaborate **Work with your partner** to complete the sentence using the correct form of **correspond** and appropriate content.

A _____ personality _____ well with a profession

such as _____ .

Your Turn **Work independently** to complete the sentence using the correct form of **correspond** and appropriate content.

How well I do on a test closely _____ to how much I _____ .

Be an Academic Author **Work independently** to write two sentences using Meaning 2. In your first sentence, use **correspond** in the *simple present tense*. In your second sentence, use **correspond** in the *simple past tense* and include the word partner.

❶ _____

_____

❷ _____

_____

> **grammar tip**
>
> **To make the simple past tense of regular verbs, add −ed or −d.**
>
> I correspond**ed** with my cousin in Laos.
>
> The store hire**d** three new clerks.

Write an Academic Paragraph **Complete** the paragraph using the correct form of **correspond** and original content.

Cognates are words in two languages that correspond in sound and meaning. For

example, the German word *Bruder* and the _____ word *brother*
                                                                ❶

are cognates. English and Spanish are two languages that have many cognates. If you

are a native English or Spanish speaker, _____ cognates can
                                                          ❷

help you learn the other _____ . Many cognates follow a pattern.
                                       ❸

For example, English adjectives that end in −*ary* often _____
                                                                      ❹

to Spanish adjectives ending in −*ario*. The English word *necessary* is *necesario* in

_____ ; *imaginary* is *imaginario*. Similarly, English nouns that end in
          ❺

−*tion* frequently _____ to Spanish nouns that end in −*ción*.
                              ❻

crisis
noun

Academic Vocabulary Toolkit

Meaning	Example
an emergency situation *Synonyms:* disaster, catastrophe	In an economic **crisis**, fewer people buy _____ items such as expensive _____ and watches.

Forms

Singular: crisis
Plural: crises

Word Partners

- economic _____
- solve a _____

During an **economic crisis**, unemployment and homelessness increase.

World leaders met in Egypt to discuss ways to **solve the crisis** in North Africa.

Verbal Practice

Talk about It **Read** each sentence and **think** about how you would complete it.

Discuss your idea with your partner using the sentence frame.

Listen carefully to your partner's and classmates' ideas.

Write your favorite idea in the blank.

❶ Recently, the world has faced numerous **crises**, including

_____ and _____ .

❷ If your family is in a **crisis**, it can be helpful to talk to a _____ .

Writing Practice

Collaborate **Work with your partner** to complete the sentence using the correct form of **crisis** and appropriate content.

Most teenagers would consider it a _____ if they got to school and realized

that they _____ .

Your Turn **Work independently** to complete the sentence using the correct form of **crisis** and appropriate content.

The person I usually turn to to help me in a _____ is _____

because _____ .

Be an Academic Author **Work independently** to write two sentences. In your first sentence, use **crisis** in the *singular form*. In your second sentence, use **crisis** in the *plural form* with the quantifier *numerous*. Use a word partner in one sentence.

❶ _____

_____

❷ _____

_____

> **grammar tip**
>
> Quantifiers are words that tell us how much or how many of something there is. They usually come before the noun they are describing.
>
> The new president faces **numerous** crises.
>
> The restaurant has **a variety of** options.

Write an Academic Paragraph **Complete** the paragraph using the correct form of **crisis** and original content.

A humanitarian crisis occurs when events such as a _____ or a
 ❶

natural disaster endanger the safety of a group of people. In the past decade, humanitarian

_____ have occurred in Haiti, Darfur, and _____ .
 ❷ ❸

Many of these _____ have resulted in large numbers of refugees fleeing
 ❹

troubled areas. During these situations, members of aid _____ , such as the
 ❺

Red Cross, bring food and _____ to help people. A humanitarian
 ❻

_____ is devastating, but in every crisis there are true heroes who put
 ❼

aside their personal safety to help others.

critical
adjective

Academic Vocabulary Toolkit

Meanings	Examples
1. pointing out problems	**1.** My sister is very **critical** of my _____ because she doesn't like how I _____ .
2. very important **Synonym:** crucial	**2.** It is **critical** that you arrive by _____ A.M. or all the _____ will be sold out.

Family

- **Verb:** criticize
- **Noun:** criticism, critic
- **Adverb:** critically

Word Partners

• _____ importance	It is of **critical importance** that you answer every question on the exam; if you leave some blank, you will not get any credit.
• _____ role	The ambassador played a **critical role** in the peace agreement between the two nations.
• highly _____	Carla is **highly critical** of how people behave on reality shows.

Verbal Practice

Talk about It   **Read** each sentence and **think** about how you would complete it.

Discuss your idea with your partner using the sentence frame.

Listen carefully to your partner's and classmates' ideas.

Write your favorite idea in the blank.

1 On the TV show _____ , the judges are not very **critical**.

2 The movie reviewer was highly **critical** of the film's _____ .

3 _____ has played a **critical** role in my education.

4 A strong _____ is of **critical** importance in an essay.

Writing Practice

Collaborate **Work with your partner** to complete the sentences using **critical** and appropriate content.

❶ Sometimes _____ is highly _____ of my schoolwork.

❷ Think hard before making a _____ decision like

_____ .

Your Turn **Work independently** to complete the sentences using **critical** and appropriate content.

❶ I am usually highly _____ of other people's _____ .

❷ A good sense of _____ is _____ if you want to be a

_____ .

Be an Academic Author **Work independently** to write two sentences. In your first sentence, use **critical** with a *singular noun*. In your second sentence, use **critical** with a word partner.

MEANING ❶ _____

_____

MEANING ❷ _____

_____

> **grammar tip**
>
> An adjective usually comes before the noun it describes.
> a <u>critical</u> issue
> a <u>big</u> house
> a <u>green</u> jacket

Write an Academic Paragraph **Complete** the paragraph using **critical** and original content.

Students sometimes complain that _____ ❶ like math and

science are a waste of time. They say they don't need math because they can simply use a

_____ ❷ and that they don't plan to be scientists. However, math and

science also teach thinking skills that are _____ ❸ to your success

in all areas of life. For example, when you _____ ❹ difficult math

problems, you not only learn math, you also learn how to work through complex issues. When

you have to redo your science _____ ❺ , you learn the importance of

_____ ❻ . These are _____ ❼ skills that benefit you

outside of the classroom as well . So, the next time you want to complain about your school's

curriculum, consider the _____ ❽ of the skills that you are learning.

crucial
adjective

Say it: **cru** • cial   **Write it:** _____

Meaning	Example	
necessary, very important **Synonym:** critical	It is **crucial** to know if you need a _____ before you travel to a _____ country.	

Family
• **Adverb:** crucially

Word Partners	
• _____ to the success of	Volunteers were **crucial to the success of** the food drive.
• play a _____ role	The actor's agent **played a crucial role** in getting him the part in the movie.

Verbal Practice

Talk about It   **Read** each sentence and **think** about how you would complete it.

Discuss your idea with your partner using the sentence frame.

Listen carefully to your partner's and classmates' ideas.

Write your favorite idea in the blank.

❶ If you are traveling in the desert, it is **crucial** that you bring

_____ .

❷ In social studies, we learned how _____ played a **crucial** role

in American history.

Writing Practice

Collaborate **Work with your partner** to complete the sentence using **crucial** and appropriate content.

One thing that is _____ to your success in this school is

_____ .

Your Turn **Work independently** to complete the sentence using **crucial** and appropriate content.

Some _____ dates in history that everyone should know are

_____ , _____ , and _____ .

Be an Academic Author **Work independently** to write two sentences. In your first sentence, use **crucial** with a *plural noun*. In your second sentence, use **crucial** with the word partner *play a crucial role.*

❶ _____

_____

❷ _____

_____

> **grammar tip**
>
> An adjective usually comes before the noun it describes.
>
> a <u>crucial</u> decision
>
> a <u>big</u> house
>
> a <u>green</u> jacket

Write an Academic Paragraph **Complete** the paragraph using **crucial** and original content.

    In today's world, everything seems to be crucially important. If your friend texts you, you feel

that it is _____ to text back immediately. If your favorite musician has a
       ❶

new song, you want to _____ it right away. When you watch the news,
       ❷

you hear about _____ evidence in court cases, crucial bills that need
       ❸

to be passed in Congress, and _____ information about tomorrow's
       ❹

weather. However, some people are adopting the "slow movement." Followers of the slow

movement feel that life should not be _____ . They don't want fast food,
       ❺

and they don't think that it is _____ to get a lot done in a short amount
       ❻

of time. Instead, they think it is _____ to relax, take your time, and enjoy
       ❼

simple things, like a walk in the _____ .
       ❽

current
adjective

▶ **Say it:** cur • rent   **Write it:** _____

Meaning	Example	
belonging to the present time *Synonym:* present	The **current** issue of _____ magazine has a picture of a _____ on the cover.	

Family

- *Adverb:* currently

Word Partners

- _____ events   I read the newspaper to find out about **current events**.
- _____ trends   One of the **current trends** in education is to use technology in the classroom.

Verbal Practice

Talk about It   **Read** each sentence and **think** about how you would complete it.

Discuss your idea with your partner using the sentence frame.

Listen carefully to your partner's and classmates' ideas.

Write your favorite idea in the blank.

❶ I usually hear about **current** events from _____ .

❷ My **current** math teacher is _____ . Last year, my math teacher was _____ .

Writing Practice

Collaborate **Work with your partner** to complete the sentence using **current** and appropriate content.

One _____ fashion trend is to wear _____ .

Your Turn **Work independently** to complete the sentence using **current** and appropriate content.

My _____ interests include _____ , but when I

was five, I was more interested in _____ .

Be an Academic Author **Work independently** to write two sentences. In your first sentence, use **current** with a *singular noun*. In your second sentence, use **current** with the word partner *current trend*.

❶ _____

_____

❷ _____

_____

> ### grammar tip
> **Adjectives do not have plural forms. Do not add an –s to adjectives when they describe plural nouns.**
>
> <u>current</u> events
>
> <u>loud</u> dogs
>
> <u>puffy</u> marshmallows

Write an Academic Paragraph **Complete** the paragraph using **current** and original content.

You might have heard adults talk about the old days when everything cost

_____ ❶ . For example, in 1980, a gallon of gas was $1.19. Currently, a

gallon of gas costs approximately _____ ❷ . Back in the 1980s, bread, movie

tickets, and even _____ ❸ were less expensive. However, today's workers

earn more money than they did in the past. In 1980, the federal minimum wage was $3.10 an

hour. The _____ ❹ federal minimum wage is $7.25. Also, a few things cost

less _____ ❺ than they did in 1980. Cell phones, computers, and televisions

are less expensive and _____ ❻ than they were in the 1980s. However, if

_____ ❼ trends are any indication, in the future, prices for most items

will increase.

deny
verb

Academic Vocabulary Toolkit

Meanings	Examples
1. to say that something is not true	1. At first, the child **denied** that he had _____ the _____ jar.
2. to not give something to someone who wants or needs it	2. The _____ **denied** their captives food and _____ .

Forms	Family
Present: I/You/We/They deny He/She/It denies **Past:** denied	• **Noun:** denial

Word Partners

• confirm or _____	The politician refused to **confirm or deny** the accusation.
• _____ someone's request	The immigration office **denied Jorge's request** for a tourist visa to visit the United States.

Verbal Practice

Talk about It **Read** each sentence and **think** about how you would complete it.

Discuss your idea with your partner using the sentence frame.

Listen carefully to your partner's and classmates' ideas.

Write your favorite idea in the blank.

❶ If someone accused me of _____ , I would **deny** it.

❷ I cannot **deny** that I sometimes eat _____ , even though they are not very healthy!

❸ Our school **denies** students entry to _____ .

❹ Some governments **deny** their citizens _____ .

Writing Practice

Collaborate **Work with your partner** to complete the sentences using the correct form of **deny** and appropriate content.

❶ The company refuses to confirm or _____ that its new product

is a _____ .

❷ My teacher _____ my request _____ .

Your Turn **Work independently** to complete the sentences using the correct form of **deny** and appropriate content.

❶ The students _____ that they _____ .

❷ My parents _____ me permission to _____ .

Be an Academic Author **Work independently** to write two sentences. In your first sentence, use **deny** in the *simple past tense*. In your second sentence, use **deny** with the adverb of frequency *usually*.

MEANING ❶ _____

_____

MEANING ❷ _____

_____

> **grammar tip**
>
> **Adverbs of frequency are words that show how often something happens. They usually go before the main verb.**
>
> My parents **usually** **deny** me permission to watch TV.
>
> You **always** **forget** something!

Write an Academic Paragraph **Complete** the paragraph using the correct form of **deny** and original content.

One of the most famous murder cases in American _____❶ was

that of Lizzie Borden. She was _____❷ of killing her father and

stepmother with an axe at their home in Fall River, Massachusetts, in 1892. Lizzie Borden

always _____❸ committing the crimes. Since neither the murder

_____❹ nor any bloody clothes were found, it was difficult to

_____❺ that Lizzie was the murderer. Furthermore, at her trial, the

judge _____❻ the prosecution permission to admit some key evidence.

Jurors never heard that Lizzie had recently tried to buy some poison. Lizzie was found not

_____❼ and lived the rest of her life in Fall River.

distinguish
verb

▶ *Say it:* dis • **tin** • guish   *Write it:* _____

Meaning	Example
to see or show a difference *Synonym:* to set apart	Because they are _____ twins, it is _____ to **distinguish** Hannah from Hailey.

Forms	Family
Present: I/You/We/They distinguish He/She/It distinguishes **Past:** distinguished	• **Adjective:** distinguishable

Word Partners	
• _____ between	Even experts can't **distinguish between** the original painting and the copy.
• _____ something from something else	I **distinguished** the Spanish team **from** the German team by the color of their uniforms.

Verbal Practice

Talk about It   **Read** each sentence and **think** about how you would complete it.

Discuss your idea with your partner using the sentence frame.

Listen carefully to your partner's and classmates' ideas.

Write your favorite idea in the blank.

❶ By the time they reach the age of _____ , children should be able to **distinguish** right from wrong.

❷ One thing that **distinguishes** me from the rest of my family is

_____ .

Writing Practice

Collaborate **Work with your partner** to complete the sentence using the correct form of **distinguish** and appropriate content.

What _____ our school from other schools is our _____ .

Your Turn **Work independently** to complete the sentence using the correct form of **distinguish** and appropriate content.

Take Nia with you when you buy jewelry because she can _____

between _____ and _____ .

Be an Academic Author **Work independently** to write two sentences. In your first sentence, use **distinguish** with the modal verb *can*. In your second sentence, use **distinguish** in the *simple present tense* with a word partner.

❶ _____

_____

❷ _____

_____

> ### grammar tip
>
> **Modal verbs are helping verbs that give additional meaning to the main verb. *Can* expresses ability.**
>
> I **can** distinguish right from wrong.
>
> He **can run** a mile in five minutes.

Write an Academic Paragraph **Complete** the paragraph using the correct form of **distinguish** and original content.

When you read, it's important to be able to _____ between fact and
❶

opinion. A _____ is something that can be proven true or false. An
❷

_____ , on the other hand, expresses a person's feelings. Sometimes
❸

it is easy to _____ fact from opinion. For example, the statement,
❹

"William Johnson was an American painter," is a fact. It can be _____ .
❺

An opinion can be easily _____ when it follows the words " "I think"
❻

or "I believe." "I think William Johnson is one of America's most important painters," is obviously an

_____ . Not all opinions are that easy to spot. For example, "Johnson's
❼

talent reached its peak in his painting *Café*," makes a _____ about Johnson
❽

and is an _____ .
❾

diverse
adjective

▶ **Say it:** **di** • verse

Write it: _____

Meaning	Example	
made up of a wide variety of things or people **Synonym:** varied	_____ is a geographically **diverse** state with deserts, forests, _____ , and valleys.	*(map of California: Mt. Shasta, Cascade Range, Sacramento Valley, Sierra Nevada, San Joaquin Valley, Mt. Whitney, Death Valley, Mojave Desert, Pacific Ocean)*

Forms	Family
diverse	• **Noun:** diversity • **Adverb:** diversely

Word Partners	
• culturally _____	Sheng's school is **culturally diverse** with students from more than 20 countries.
• _____ group	Marco has a **diverse group** of friends; some are on the basketball team and others are in the drama club.

Verbal Practice

Talk about It   **Read** each sentence and **think** about how you would complete it.

Discuss your idea with your partner using the sentence frame.

Listen carefully to your partner's and classmates' ideas.

Write your favorite idea in the blank.

❶ One way that students in our school are **diverse** is that they

_____ .

❷ Students in this class have **diverse** musical tastes; we like everything from

_____ to _____ .

64

Writing Practice

Collaborate Work with your partner to complete the sentence using **diverse** and appropriate content.

The United States is becoming more and more culturally _____

every year as people immigrate here from countries such as _____

and _____ .

Your Turn Work independently to complete the sentence using **diverse** and appropriate content.

I have _____ interests, including _____ and

_____ .

Be an Academic Author Work independently to write two sentences. In your first sentence, use **diverse** with a *plural noun*. In your second sentence, use **diverse** with the word partner *culturally diverse*.

❶ _____

_____

❷ _____

_____

> ## grammar tip
>
> An adjective usually come befores the noun it modifies.
>
> a <u>diverse</u> community
>
> a <u>big</u> house
>
> a <u>green</u> jacket

Write an Academic Paragraph **Complete** the paragraph using **diverse** and original content.

You don't have to look far to find a place with a lot of diversity: your school! Today's

schools are _____ in a number of ways. Many schools are
        ❶

_____ diverse; students might come from many different countries
     ❷

and speak many different _____ . Even when a school is not culturally
         ❸

_____ , students are still a diverse group of people. Every class has a wide
    ❹

range of personalities and _____ . Some students are calm and easy-
        ❺

going, while others are more _____ . Students also have a diverse range
      ❻

of talents and _____ . This diversity enriches every student's experience
     ❼

and makes school a more interesting place to be.

diversity
noun

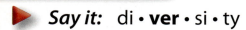

Say it: di • **ver** • si • ty   **Write it:** _____

Academic Vocabulary Toolkit

Meaning	Example	
a wide variety of things or people **Synonym:** variety	New York City is famous for its _____ diversity; all kinds of people live in its _____ neighborhoods.	

Family

- **Verb:** diversify
- **Adjective:** diverse
- **Adverb:** diversely

Word Partners

• ethnic _____	There isn't a lot of **ethnic diversity** in Japan; almost everyone is Japanese.
• _____ of opinion	The editorial page should include a **diversity of opinion**, not just one person's thoughts.

Verbal Practice

Talk about It **Read** each sentence and **think** about how you would complete it.

Discuss your idea with your partner using the sentence frame.

Listen carefully to your partner's and classmates' ideas.

Write your favorite idea in the blank.

❶ Our community's **diversity** can be seen in its wide variety of

_____ .

❷ If you want to hear a **diversity** of opinion, just go to _____ .

66

Writing Practice

Collaborate **Work with your partner** to complete the sentence using **diversity** and appropriate content.

Sometimes people complain that there is not enough _____ in certain professions such as _____ .

Your Turn **Work independently** to complete the sentence using **diversity** and appropriate content.

When people talk about topics such as _____ , there is often a great _____ of opinion.

Be an Academic Author **Work independently** to write two sentences. In your first sentence, use **diversity** with the word partner *diversity of opinion*. In your second sentence, use **diversity** with the word partner *ethnic diversity*.

❶ _____

_____

❷ _____

_____

> ### grammar tip
> An adjective usually comes before the noun it describes.
> <u>ethnic</u> diversity
> a <u>big</u> house
> a <u>green</u> jacket

Write an Academic Paragraph **Complete** the paragraph using the correct form of **diversity** and original content.

Most people enjoy visiting zoos to see the _____ ❶ of wildlife inside. However, some people dislike zoos because they believe that _____ ❷ belong in their natural environment and that it is cruel to keep them in cages. They believe that zoos are unnatural and _____ ❸ for animals. In response, animal experts and advocates _____ ❹ that many modern zoos actually work to save animals that are in danger of _____ ❺ . Zoos breed these animals in order to increase their _____ ❻ and save the species' future. Today, as many animals and environments face great danger, zoos are actually helping to maintain the Earth's biological _____ ❼ .

element
noun

▶ **Say it:** el • e • ment   **Write it:** _____

Meaning	Example
a part or a small amount of something **Synonyms:** component, ingredient	_____ is an important **element** of any _____ program.

Forms	Family
Singular: element **Plural:** elements	**Adjective:** elemental

Word Partners
• essential _____   Art and music are **essential elements** in the development of children.
• key _____   A **key element** of a good education is having teachers who care about their students.

Verbal Practice

Talk about It   **Read** each sentence and **think** about how you would complete it.

Discuss your idea with your partner using the sentence frame.

Listen carefully to your partner's and classmates' ideas.

Write your favorite idea in the blank.

❶ The key **elements** of a good movie are a great story and _____ .

❷ If you want to learn the basic **elements** of a language, the best way to start is to _____ .

Writing Practice

Collaborate **Work with your partner** to complete the sentence using the correct form of **element** and appropriate content.

_____ is an essential _____ in building a relationship with

_____ .

Your Turn **Work independently** to complete the sentence using the correct form of **element** and appropriate content.

In a _____ , several _____ join together to form something

beautiful.

Be an **Work independently** to write two sentences. In your first sentence, use **element** in the *singular form*
Academic and include a word partner. In your second sentence, use **element** in the *plural form* with the quantifier
Author *several*.

❶ _____

_____

❷ _____

_____

> ### grammar tip
>
> Quantifiers are words that tell us how much or how many of something there is. They usually come before the noun they are describing.
>
> I liked <u>several</u> **elements** of his new designs.
>
> <u>All</u> **the students** had pizza for lunch.

Write an **Complete** the paragraph using the correct form of **element** and original
Academic content.
Paragraph

You know a good story when you read one. What are some of the essential ingredients,

or _____ , of a good story? Many writers say their stories begin
            ❶

with the main character. In all stories, this central _____ , often
                                        ❷

called the protagonist, faces a problem. How the _____ solves the
                                       ❸

problem is the key _____ of the story's plot. Another important
                ❹

_____ of any story is its setting. The setting of a story includes the time
    ❺

and the _____ where the story happens. Writers use the framework
        ❻

of a story to explore important themes, or ideas. Some major themes in literature include the

conflict between the individual and _____ or the struggle between
                                    ❼

humans and _____ .
            ❽

69

eliminate
verb

Say it: e • **lim** • i • nate   Write it: _____

Meaning	Example
to get rid of something **Synonyms:** remove, erase	The Salk and Sabin _____ have almost completely **eliminated** the _____ virus in industrialized countries.

Forms	Family
Present: I/You/We/They eliminate He/She/It eliminates **Past:** eliminated	• **Noun:** elimination • **Adjective:** eliminated

Word Partners	
• completely _____	According to the plan, Europe will **completely eliminate** carbon emissions by 2050.
• _____ the need for	Debit and credit card scanners will gradually **eliminate the need for** cash.
• _____ the possibility	New rules **eliminate the possibility** of tie games.

Verbal Practice

Talk about It   **Read** each sentence and **think** about how you would complete it.

Discuss your idea with your partner using the sentence frame.

Listen carefully to your partner's and classmates' ideas.

Write your favorite idea in the blank.

❶ New smart phones **eliminate** the need for _____ .

❷ The best way to **eliminate** stress from your life is to _____ .

Writing Practice

Collaborate **Work with your partner** to complete the sentence using the correct form of **eliminate** and appropriate content.

Failing biology has _____ the possibility that I will _____ .

Your Turn **Work independently** to complete the sentence using the correct form of **eliminate** and appropriate content.

When taking a multiple-choice _____ , a good strategy is to

_____ the answers that are obviously wrong and then _____

the best answer from the remaining choices.

Be an Academic Author **Work independently** to write two sentences. In your first sentence, use **eliminate** in the *present perfect tense*. In your second sentence, use **eliminate** in the *simple present tense* and include a word partner.

❶ _____

_____

❷ _____

_____

> ## grammar tip
>
> The present perfect tense is formed with *has/have* + the past participle form of the verb. To make the past participle of regular verbs, add *–ed* or *-d*.
>
> I have eliminat**ed** soda from my diet.
>
> She has play**ed** tennis for many years.

Write an Academic Paragraph **Complete** the paragraph using the correct form of **eliminate** and original content.

A new system of personal identification could soon _____ the
                                                              ❶
need for house keys and computer passwords. This system, known as biometrics, relies

on fingerprint or eye scans to _____ people. To unlock a door
                                        ❷
or _____ a computer, users have to scan either a fingerprint
        ❸
or their eye. Some companies have already started selling house locks that allow

_____ to program in their fingerprints. Imagine: you would never
        ❹
accidentally _____ yourself out of your house again! Biometric devices
                     ❺
for personal computers could also _____ the threat of identity theft
                                            ❻
since fingerprints and the iris pattern of the eye are _____ and cannot
                                                                ❼
be hacked.

71

enable
verb

▶ **Say it:** en • **a** • ble   **Write it:** _____

Meaning	Example
to make something possible **Synonyms:** allow, help **Antonym:** disable	Chrissie's _____ eye surgery will **enable** her to see without _____ .

Forms		Family
Present: I/You/We/They enable He/She/It enables		• **Adjective:** enabling
Past: enabled		

Verbal Practice

Talk about It   **Read** each sentence and **think** about how you would complete it.

Discuss your idea with your partner using the sentence frame.

Listen carefully to your partner's and classmates' ideas.

Write your favorite idea in the blank.

❶ Internet access **enables** us to _____ .

❷ _____ **enable** us to move quickly from one place to another.

Writing Practice

Collaborate **Work with your partner** to complete the sentence using the correct form of **enable** and appropriate content.

Someday, scientists will invent a _____ that will _____

us to _____ .

Your Turn **Work independently** to complete the sentence using the correct form of **enable** and appropriate content.

My high school education will _____ me to _____ .

Be an Academic Author **Work independently** to write two sentences. In your first sentence, use **enable** in the *simple present tense*. In your second sentence, use **enable** with the modal verb *will*.

❶ _____

_____

❷ _____

_____

Write an Academic Paragraph **Complete** the paragraph using the correct form of **enable** and original content.

Ants have a special ridged organ built into their abdomens that _____

❶

them to make sounds. Ants make these sounds to _____ with

❷

each other. The queen ant uses this technique to give commands that the worker ants

_____ . Recent developments in audio technology have

❸

_____ scientists to observe and listen to the ants. Scientists placed tiny

❹

microphones and speakers into the ants' nests and were able to _____

❺

and play back the sounds made by queen ants. The worker ants responded to the sounds from

the speakers and followed the _____ ! Scientists also found that other

❻

species have learned the ants' _____ and use it to make the ants do

❼

things for them, such as feed and protect their babies.

exclude
verb

Say it: ex • **clude**   **Write it:** _____

Academic Vocabulary Toolkit

Meaning	Example
to leave someone or something out **Synonyms:** omit, keep out **Antonym:** include	The _____ boys **excluded** Jimmy from the game because he was too _____ .

Forms

Present:	
I/You/We/They	exclude
He/She/It	excludes
Past:	excluded

Family

- **Noun:** exclusion
- **Adjective:** exclusive
- **Adverb:** exclusively
- **Preposition:** excluding

Word Partners

- _____ the possibility   Police are not **excluding the possibility** of murder in their investigation into the death of Mrs. Norris.

Verbal Practice

Talk about It **Read** each sentence and **think** about how you would complete it.

Discuss your idea with your partner using the sentence frame.

Listen carefully to your partner's and classmates' ideas.

Write your favorite idea in the blank.

❶ I don't know who is responsible for _____ , but I am **excluding** the possibility that it was aliens from outer space.

❷ It's unfair to **exclude** certain people from a school or job based on _____ .

Writing Practice

Collaborate   **Work with your partner** to complete the sentence using the correct form of **exclude** and appropriate content.

If you're writing a research paper for school, you should _____ opinions that

you can't support with _____ .

Your Turn   **Work independently** to complete the sentence using the correct form of **exclude** and appropriate content.

We don't know how the _____ team will do this year, but after today's loss we

can _____ the possibility of them _____ .

Be an Academic Author   **Work independently** to write two sentences. In your first sentence, use **exclude** with the modal verb *should*. In your second sentence, use **exclude** in the *present progressive tense*. Include the word partner *exclude the possibility* in one sentence.

❶ _____

_____

❷ _____

_____

> ### grammar tip
>
> **Modal verbs are helping verbs that give additional meaning to the main verb.** *Should* **expresses advice.**
>
> You **should** **exclude** opinions from your research paper.
>
> He **should** **eat** more vegetables.

Write an Academic Paragraph   **Complete** the paragraph using the correct form of **exclude** and original content.

In the United States, as in other democratic nations, voters _____

❶

leaders to represent them in government. Yet many voters cannot answer even basic

_____ about current issues or how our government works.

❷

Should the government _____ people to take a test about the

❸

U.S. government and _____ when they register to vote? Some

❹

argue that this would be a reasonable way to _____ uninformed

❺

people from voting. However, others _____ that no test could

❻

accurately and fairly measure how informed a person is. Who would come up with the

test? It is _____ that the test could be written in such a way as to

❼

_____ certain groups of people from voting.

❽

expand
verb

▶ **Say it:** ex • **pand** **Write it:** _____

Academic Vocabulary Toolkit

Meanings	Examples
1. to grow larger, increase *Synonyms:* grow, spread out	1. Sophie **expanded** her _____ business and moved to a new _____ .
2. to explain or add more details (always used with *on*) *Synonym:* elaborate	2. The _____ asked the candidate to **expand** on her statement.

Forms	Family
Present: I/You/We/They expand He/She/It expands **Past:** expanded	• **Noun:** expansion • **Adjective:** expansive • **Adverb:** expansively

Word Partners

• _____ and contract	Heat and cold cause things to **expand and contract**.
• _____ (my/your/his/her/its/ our/their) business	More advertising will help the company **expand its business**.

Verbal Practice

Talk about It **Read** each sentence and **think** about how you would complete it.

Discuss your idea with your partner using the sentence frame.

Listen carefully to your partner's and classmates' ideas.

Write your favorite idea in the blank.

❶ Our town is **expanding** so fast we need to

_____ .

❷ You can **expand** your vocabulary by _____ .

❸ I **expanded** on the topic by adding more _____ .

❹ In his solo, the musician took the _____ and **expanded** on it.

Writing Practice

Collaborate   **Work with your partner** to complete the sentence using the correct form of **expand** and appropriate content.

❶ The new government program aims to _____ the number of people who

_____ .

❷ Advanced biology _____ on what we learned in _____.

Your Turn   **Work independently** to complete the sentences using the correct form of **expand** and appropriate content.

❶ Our lungs _____ and contract when we _____ in and out.

❷ I will go back and _____ on what I said in my _____ .

Be an Academic Author   **Work independently** to write two sentences. In your first sentence, use **expand** in the *present progressive tense* and include a word partner. In your second sentence, use **expand** with the modal verb *could*.

MEANING **❶** _____

_____

MEANING **❷** _____

_____

> ### grammar tip
>
> **The present progressive tense is formed with *am/is/are* + a verb ending in *–ing*.**
>
> He **is expanding** his garden so he can grow corn.
>
> I **am acting** in the play.

Write an Academic Paragraph   **Complete** the paragraph using the correct form of **expand** and original content.

Cosmologists, scientists who study the universe, say the universe is expanding.

Most scientists once _____ that the universe was stable; it was
❶

neither contracting nor _____ . However, the discoveries of
❷

Edwin Hubble changed everything. Hubble studied the movement of nearby galaxies.

He _____ that other galaxies were moving away from us. The
❸

_____ that are the farthest away are moving the fastest. In fact,
❹

everything in the universe is moving _____ from everything else.
❺

Scientists believe this expansion has been happening since the _____
❻

began and that the universe will continue to _____ forever.
❼

factual
adjective

▶ **Say it:** **fac** • tu • al   **Write it:** _____

Meaning	Example
based on facts **Synonym:** true	A **factual** _____ about me is that I have a great _____ .

Family

- **Noun:** fact
- **Adverb:** factually

Word Partners

• _____ errors	Newspapers have a fact-checking team that checks articles for **factual errors**.
• _____ information	She looked online for **factual information** on the topic.

Verbal Practice

Talk about It   **Read** each sentence and **think** about how you would complete it.

Discuss your idea with your partner using the sentence frame.

Listen carefully to your partner's and classmates' ideas.

Write your favorite idea in the blank.

❶ When you are writing a _____ , it's important to keep it **factual**; you shouldn't add your _____ .

❷ Although the movie _____ is based on a true story, it has many **factual** errors.

Writing Practice

Collaborate   **Work with your partner** to complete the sentence using **factual** and appropriate content.

When I want to find _____ information for a paper, I usually look _____ .

Your Turn   **Work independently** to complete the sentence using **factual** and appropriate content.

Here is one _____ statement about me: I am _____ .

Be an Academic Author   **Work independently** to write two sentences. In your first sentence, use **factual** with a *plural noun*. In your second sentence, use **factual** with the word partner *information*.

❶ _____

_____

❷ _____

_____

> **grammar tip**
>
> An adjective usually comes before the noun it describes.
>
> **factual** information
>
> the **big** house
>
> a **green** jacket

Write an Academic Paragraph   **Complete** the paragraph using **factual** and original content.

In school, students are often asked to find _____ information about a
❶

famous person in history, such as Martin Luther King Jr. or _____ .
❷

To find this information, students might read a biography or an autobiography. An

autobiography is different from a _____ in that it is written
❸

by the person it is about. Students might also read a memoir. A memoir is a kind

of _____ . In a memoir, the _____ tells the story
❹   ❺

of a specific time in his or her life. Memoirs, like biographies and _____ ,
❻

are supposed to be factual; but, of course, _____ sometimes slip in. It
❼

may be impossible to be completely _____ when you write about the
❽

past. Memory cannot always be trusted.

feature
noun

▶ **Say it:** fea • ture   **Write it:** _____

<table>
<tr><th colspan="2">Meaning</th><th colspan="2">Example</th></tr>
<tr><td colspan="2">an important part or a special characteristic</td><td colspan="2">The latest laptop has several _____ new **features** that are sure to make it very _____ .</td></tr>
</table>

Academic Vocabulary Toolkit

Forms	Family
• *Singular:* feature • *Plural:* features	• *Verb:* feature • *Adjective:* featured

Word Partners	
• key _____	**Key features** of a good Internet service provider are speed and dependability.
• common _____	There are different kinds of penguins, but all penguins share some **common features**.
• central _____	A large fountain is the **central feature** of the park.

Verbal Practice

Talk about It **Read** each sentence and **think** about how you would complete it.

Discuss your idea with your partner using the sentence frame.

Listen carefully to your partner's and classmates' ideas.

Write your favorite idea in the blank.

❶ My phone has a several special **features**, including _____ .

❷ A common **feature** of mammals is that they

_____ .

Writing Practice

Collaborate **Work with your partner** to complete the sentence using the correct form of **feature** and appropriate content.

A key _____ of a successful rock band is a _____ .

Your Turn **Work independently** to complete the sentence using the correct form of **feature** and appropriate content.

The central _____ of the geography of _____ is

_____ .

Be an Academic Author **Work independently** to write two sentences. In your first sentence, use **feature** in the *singular form* and include a word partner. In your second sentence, use **feature** in the *plural form* with the quantifier *several*.

❶ _____

_____

❷ _____

_____

> ### grammar tip
>
> Quantifiers are words that tell us how much or how many of something there is. They usually come before the noun they are describing.
>
> My phone has **several features** I don't use.
>
> This quiz has **many questions**.

Write an Academic Paragraph **Complete** the paragraph using the correct form of **feature** and original content.

Almost one-third of the Earth's land is desert or semidesert. Deserts are dry regions

with unusual _____ not found anywhere else. The surface
                              ❶

of a _____ can be bare rock, a dry plain covered with small
             ❷

rocks, or sand. Sand dunes are one of the most common and most recognizable desert

_____ . Because deserts are so _____ ,
          ❸   ❹

not many plants can grow there. With very few _____ to hold
                                                        ❺

the soil, deserts are subject to erosion, a slow wearing away of land. Erosion in the

_____ forms interesting geological _____ ,
          ❻   ❼

such as mesas—large hills with flat tops—and hoodoos, which are odd-shaped columns or

piles of stones.

focus
noun

Say it: **fo** • cus   Write it: _____

Meaning	Example
the attention that you give to something	My sister is taking many different classes at college, like literature and _____ ; but her main **focus** is on _____ .
Synonym: emphasis	

Forms	Family
• **Singular:** focus • **Plural:** focuses or foci	• **Verb:** focus • **Adjective:** focused

Word Partners
• main _____   My **main focus** this week will be preparing for the 5K race on Sunday.
• primary _____   It's Mother's Day, so our **primary focus** is on doing nice things for mom.
• lose _____   The quarterback **lost focus** on the field and threw for an interception.

Verbal Practice

Talk about It **Read** each sentence and **think** about how you would complete it.

Discuss your idea with your partner using the sentence frame.

Listen carefully to your partner's and classmates' ideas.

Write your favorite idea in the blank.

❶ The **focus** of the news last week was _____ .

❷ Right now, the main **focus** of my life is _____ .

Writing Practice

Collaborate **Work with your partner** to complete the sentence using **focus** and appropriate content.

The primary _____ of a professional _____

should be _____ .

Your Turn **Work independently** to complete the sentence using **focus** and appropriate content.

When I play _____ , I can usually win if I don't lose my _____ .

Be an Academic Author **Work independently** to write two sentences. In your first sentence, use **focus** with the word partner *main focus*. In your second sentence, use **focus** with the word partner *lose focus*.

❶ _____

_____

❷ _____

_____

> **grammar tip**
>
> Although *focus* is not often used in the plural, it has two different plural forms! Both *focuses* and *foci* are acceptable plural forms of *focus*.

Write an Academic Paragraph **Complete** the paragraph using **focus** and original content.

In the United States, we put a lot of _____ on work—maybe
❶

too much! Americans have a strong work ethic, and we _____
❷

people who work hard. However, we barely rest! Many people in the United States get

no paid _____ at all. Americans who do have paid vacation time
❸

take only an average of 12 days per _____ . In Japan and Korea,
❹

_____ get 25 days of vacation; in France, they get 37; and in Italy, they
❺

get 42! This time allows people to focus more on their _____ and on
❻

enjoying themselves. It's not that American workers wouldn't like more vacation time. Most

people would like to shift at least some of their _____ from work to
❼

leisure time.

function
noun

Academic Vocabulary Toolkit

Meaning	Example
the thing that something is supposed to do *Synonyms:* use, purpose	Shutters may be _____ , but they can also perform the **function** of keeping out _____ .

Forms	Family
• *Singular:* function • *Plural:* functions	• *Verb:* function • *Adjective:* functioning, functional

Word Partners	
• primary _____	The **primary function** of a ceiling fan is to cool a room in the summer, but it can also push heat down from the ceiling in the winter.
• perform the _____ of	The vice president will **perform the functions of** the president if the president is ill.

Verbal Practice

Talk about It   **Read** each sentence and **think** about how you would complete it.

Discuss your idea with your partner using the sentence frame.

Listen carefully to your partner's and classmates' ideas.

Write your favorite idea in the blank.

❶ I think the **function** of dreams is to _____ .

❷ The primary **function** of education is to _____ .

Writing Practice

Collaborate | **Work with your partner** to complete the sentence using the correct form of **function** and appropriate content.

Two main _____ of government are to _____

and _____ .

Your Turn | **Work independently** to complete the sentence using the correct form of **function** and appropriate content.

If you don't have any tools, you might be able to use a _____ to perform

the _____ of a _____ .

Be an Academic Author | **Work independently** to write two sentences. In your first sentence, use **function** in the *singular form* and include a word partner. In your second sentence, use **function** in the *plural form*.

❶ _____

_____

❷ _____

_____

> **grammar tip**
>
> Count nouns name things that can be counted. Count nouns have two forms, singular and plural. To make most count nouns plural, add –s.
> The human liver has several function**s**.
> He likes board game**s**.

Write an Academic Paragraph | **Complete** the paragraph using the correct form of **function** and original content.

The human body is made up of different systems. These _____ ❶

include the respiratory system, the nervous system, the skeletal and muscular

systems, as well as _____ ❷ others. The systems are constantly

_____ ❸ with each other. Each system does, however, have a specific

purpose or _____ ❹ . For example, the function of the respiratory

system is to take in oxygen and _____ ❺ carbon dioxide. The skeletal

and muscular systems include all of the body's bones and _____ ❻ . The

_____ ❼ of these systems are to protect the body and allow it to move.

For the body to work, all systems must be performing their _____ ❽ .

fundamental
adjective

Academic Vocabulary Toolkit

Meaning	Example
basic and important **Synonyms:** essential, central	Reading is **fundamental** to _____ in modern _____ .

Family

- **Noun:** fundamental
- **Adverb:** fundamentally

Word Partners

• _____ difference	The **fundamental difference** between a Spanish tortilla and a Mexican tortilla is that the first is made with eggs and the second with ground corn.
• _____ right	In a democracy, people have a **fundamental right** to free speech.
• _____ question	Scientists are still seeking the answers for **fundamental questions** about the universe.

Verbal Practice

Talk about It **Read** each sentence and **think** about how you would complete it.

Discuss your idea with your partner using the sentence frame.

Listen carefully to your partner's and classmates' ideas.

Write your favorite idea in the blank.

❶ There are **fundamental** differences between _____

and _____ .

❷ Humans have a **fundamental** right to _____ .

Writing Practice

Collaborate   **Work with your partner** to complete the sentence using **fundamental** and appropriate content.

Before we can make changes at our school, we need to ask _____ questions like,

_____

Your Turn   **Work independently** to complete the sentence using **fundamental** and appropriate content.

Children have _____ rights to a safe home and a

_____ .

Be an Academic Author   **Work independently** to write two sentences. In your first sentence, use **fundamental** with a *singular noun*. In your second sentence, use **fundamental** with a *plural noun*. Include a word partner in one sentence.

❶ _____

_____

❷ _____

_____

> **grammar tip**
>
> Adjectives do not have plural forms. Do not add an –s to adjectives when they describe plural nouns.
>
> <u>fundamental</u> differences
> <u>loud</u> dogs

Write an Academic Paragraph   **Complete** the paragraph using **fundamental** and original content.

One _____ ❶ characteristic of all poetry is that it is expressive. It

uses words and imagery to describe people, things, and _____ ❷ and

to capture and convey emotions. *Lyric poetry* expresses personal and emotional feelings.

It usually has a set rhythm and words that _____ ❸ at the end of its

lines. *Epic poetry*, on the other hand, usually describes a _____ ❹ event

like a battle or an adventure. *Free verse* is fundamentally different from the other types of

_____ ❺ because it has no rules or fixed structure. There are many more

_____ ❻ of poetry. Poetry is a _____ ❼ means of

human expression; it is as varied and rich as humanity itself!

generalization
noun

Say it: gen • er • al • i • **za** • tion   **Write it:** _____

Meaning	Example
a statement about something that is based on limited facts and which may be only partly or sometimes true	When a group of boys made the **generalization** that _____ can't hit a ball, the girl's _____ team challenged the boys to a competition.

Forms	Family
• **Singular:** generalization • **Plural:** generalizations	• **Verb:** generalize

Word Partners

• broad _____	It's a **broad generalization** to say that all college students are rich.
• make _____	When you only know one person from a different country, it's hard not to **make generalizations** about that culture based on the person.

Verbal Practice

Talk about It   **Read** each sentence and **think** about how you would complete it.

Discuss your idea with your partner using the sentence frame.

Listen carefully to your partner's and classmates' ideas.

Write your favorite idea in the blank.

❶ If I had to make a **generalization** about the weather in this area, I would say

_____ .

❷ I agree with the **generalization** about babies that they

_____ .

Writing Practice

Collaborate **Work with your partner** to complete the sentence using the correct form of **generalization** and appropriate content.

She often makes _____ about people that turn out to be

_____ .

Your Turn **Work independently** to complete the sentence using the correct form of **generalization** and appropriate content.

One broad _____ about teenagers is that they are _____ .

Be an Academic Author **Work independently** to write two sentences. In your first sentence, use **generalization** in the *singular form*. In your second sentence, use **generalization** in the *plural form* and include a word partner.

❶ _____

_____

❷ _____

_____

> ### grammar tip
>
> Count nouns name things that can be counted. Count nouns have two forms, singular and plural. To make most count nouns plural, add –s.
>
> Some generalizations may be true.
>
> He likes to play board games.

Write an Academic Paragraph **Complete** the paragraph using the correct form of **generalization** and original content.

    Generalizations may or may not be true, but you should avoid them when you write. Why

are _____ so bad? Broad _____ will make
       ❶   ❷

your readers stop reading. Readers know that statements like "Teenagers spend all their money

on clothes and music" can't possibly be _____ . Say things like that,
                                         ❸

and _____ will no longer believe anything that you've written. How
     ❹

can you avoid _____ in your writing? First of all, be specific. Instead
           ❺

of saying, "Teenagers spend all their money on clothes and music," say something like,

"_____ teenagers spend a large percentage of their money on clothes
   ❻

and music." Even better, do some research. Facts and _____ will convince
                                              ❼

readers when a generalization never would.

imply
verb

▶ **Say it:** im • **ply**   **Write it:** _____

<table>
<tr><td colspan="2">Meaning</td><td colspan="2">Example</td></tr>
<tr><td colspan="2">to suggest something without saying it directly

Synonym: hint at</td><td colspan="2">Without actually saying so, the commercial implies that this new _____ will make you _____ .</td></tr>
</table>

Forms		Family
Present:		• **Noun:** implication
I/You/We/They imply		• **Adjective:** implied
He/She/It implies		
Past: implied		

Word Partners

• mean to _____   When you gave me soap for a present, did you **mean to imply** I needed a bath?

• seem to _____   His chest pain **seemed to imply** he was having a heart attack.

Verbal Practice

Talk about It **Read** each sentence and **think** about how you would complete it.

Discuss your idea with your partner using the sentence frame.

Listen carefully to your partner's and classmates' ideas.

Write your favorite idea in the blank.

❶ When a teacher tells a student to spend more time on homework, she might be **implying** that _____ .

❷ Although the writer never said so directly, the article in the school paper seemed to **imply** that the food at our cafeteria was _____ .

Writing Practice

Collaborate **Work with your partner** to complete the sentence using the correct form of **imply** and appropriate content.

Through the clever use of statistics, the writer _____ something that was not

actually _____ .

Your Turn **Work independently** to complete the sentence using the correct form of **imply** and appropriate content.

When I said you should get some new _____ , I didn't mean to

_____ that you are _____ .

Be an Academic Author **Work independently** to write two sentences. In your first sentence, use **imply** in the *simple past tense*. In your second sentence, use **imply** with a word partner.

❶ _____

_____

❷ _____

_____

> **grammar tip**
>
> **To form the simple past tense of verbs that end in a consonant + *y*, change the *y* to *i* and add –*ed*.**
>
> He impli**ed** that he was rich.
>
> Sofia tri**ed** her best to get an A.

Write an Academic Paragraph **Complete** the paragraph using the correct form of **imply** and original content.

Companies spend _____ of dollars in advertising to promote their
                                    ❶

products. Some of this money goes to paying celebrities to appear in commercials. Advertisers

like celebrities because, for many people, celebrity _____ success. A cell
                                                                        ❷

phone commercial, for example, with a celebrity such as _____ seems to
                                                                               ❸

_____ that if you buy this cell phone, you will be rich and famous too.
          ❹

Advertising companies are very careful about the _____ they choose to
                                                                       ❺

represent their product. The wrong celebrity can send the wrong message about their product.

A celebrity who is too young may imply that the product is not _____ .
                                                                                    ❻

A celebrity who is too old may _____ that the product is not modern
                                             ❼

or stylish.

infer
verb

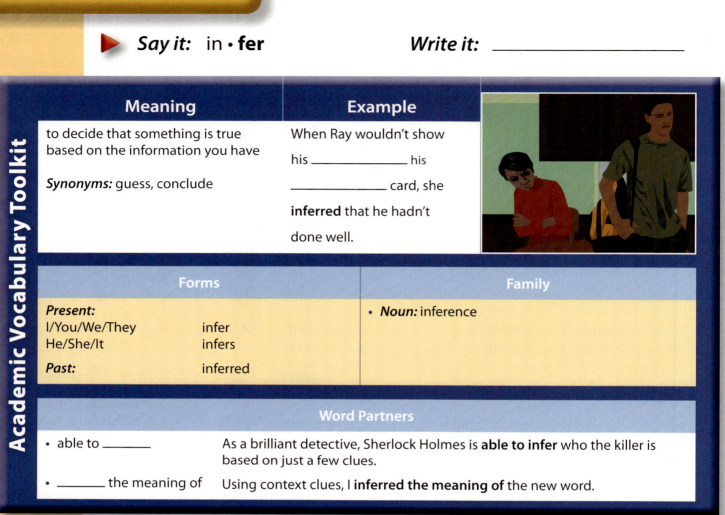

Academic Vocabulary Toolkit

Meaning	Example
to decide that something is true based on the information you have	When Ray wouldn't show his _____ his _____ card, she **inferred** that he hadn't done well.
Synonyms: guess, conclude	

Forms		Family
Present:		• **Noun:** inference
I/You/We/They	infer	
He/She/It	infers	
Past:	inferred	

Word Partners	
• able to _____	As a brilliant detective, Sherlock Holmes is **able to infer** who the killer is based on just a few clues.
• _____ the meaning of	Using context clues, I **inferred the meaning of** the new word.

Verbal Practice

Talk about It **Read** each sentence and **think** about how you would complete it.

Discuss your idea with your partner using the sentence frame.

Listen carefully to your partner's and classmates' ideas.

Write your favorite idea in the blank.

❶ When the baseball team came into the ice-cream store looking happy, we **inferred** that _____ .

❷ If the principal calls a student to the office, the class might **infer** that the student _____ .

Writing Practice

Collaborate   **Work with your partner** to complete the sentence using the correct form of **infer** and appropriate content.

To _____ the meaning of an unknown word, it's helpful

_____ .

Your Turn   **Work independently** to complete the sentence using the correct form of **infer** and appropriate content.

From the look on my friend's face, I was able to _____ that

_____ .

Be an Academic Author   **Work independently** to write two sentences. In your first sentence, use **infer** in the *simple past tense*. In your second sentence, use **infer** with a word partner.

❶ _____

_____

❷ _____

_____

> ### grammar tip
>
> **To form the past tense of a two-syllable verb that ends in a consonant-vowel-consonant, double the final consonant and add *–ed* only if the last syllable is stressed.**
>
> Mia infer**red** the store was closed when no one answered the phone.
>
> The police permit**ted** us to close the street for our block party.

Write an Academic Paragraph   **Complete** the paragraph using the correct form of the word **infer** and original content.

It can be fascinating to think about what the world was like

_____ years ago. Of course, no one is here
❶

to tell us what _____ was really like. However, archaeologists,
❷

people who study the life and culture of people who lived long ago, can tell us a lot.

Archaeologists study artifacts, objects made by people in the past, to make inferences

about what _____ was like. For example, when archaeologists find
❸

Chinese pottery in Greece, they can reasonably _____ that there
❹

was some trade between the two cultures. If an area has a lot of jewelry, it is possible to

_____ that it was an important place. Hundreds of years from now,
❺

_____ might study the area where you live. What artifacts will they find?
❻

What will they _____ about our lives today?
❼

inference
noun

Write it: _____

Academic Vocabulary Toolkit

Meaning	Example
an opinion or guess that is based on what you already know	A good _____ looks at _____ and makes **inferences** based on them.

Forms	Family
• *Singular:* inference • *Plural:* inferences	• *Verb:* infer

Word Partners

• draw _____	Based on the information in the graph, the class **drew the inference** that world hunger is increasing.
• logical _____	The chimps made the **logical inference** that food was more likely to be found under a slanted board than under a board that was flat on the ground.
• make _____	Use what you already know to **make inferences** about what a character in a story might do.

Verbal Practice

Talk about It **Read** each sentence and **think** about how you would complete it.

Discuss your idea with your partner using the sentence frame.

Listen carefully to your partner's and classmates' ideas.

Write your favorite idea in the blank.

❶ When you read a book, you make many **inferences** based on

_____ .

❷ We used what we knew about our friends to make **inferences** about

_____ .

Writing Practice

Collaborate **Work with your partner** to complete the sentence using the correct form of **inference** and appropriate content.

If someone doesn't respond to your texts, you can draw the _____ that

_____ .

Your Turn **Work independently** to complete the sentence using the correct form of **inference** and appropriate content.

When _____ don't have all the facts, they use

_____ to make logical _____ .

Be an Academic Author **Work independently** to write two sentences. In your first sentence, use **inference** in the *singular form* and include a word partner. In your second sentence, use **inference** in the *plural form* with the quantifier *many*.

❶ _____

_____

❷ _____

_____

> ### grammar tip
>
> **Quantifiers are words that tell us how much or how many of something there is. They usually come before the noun they are describing.**
>
> I can draw <u>**many**</u> **inferences** from this chart.
>
> He has <u>**several**</u> **coins** in his pocket.

Write an Academic Paragraph **Complete** the paragraph using the correct form of **inference** and original content.

In English class, you may learn about making inferences based on what you

_____ . Making _____ is an important skill for
       ❶   ❷

many subjects. In science, you need to make logical _____ based on
                                       ❸

the results of experiments. In history class, you draw _____ about why
                                       ❹

people reacted the way they did at certain periods in time. Making inferences is also something

you do in your everyday life. For example, if you come into a classroom, and your teacher looks

angry, you might infer that he or she is _____ . When you see two people
                                       ❺

holding hands, you will probably infer that they _____ . So, when it's
                                       ❻

time to study making inferences in _____ class, remember, you do it all
                                   ❼

the time!

influence
verb

▶ **Say it:** **in** · flu · ence   ***Write it:*** _____

Meaning	Example	
to affect someone or something **Synonym:** change	Tunisia's _____ in 2010 **influenced** other countries in the _____ , such as Egypt.	

Forms		Family
Present: I/You/We/They influence He/She/It influences **Past:** influenced		• **Noun:** influence • **Adjective:** influential • **Adverb:** influentially

Word Partners

• _____ behavior	We are not always aware of how advertising **influences behavior**.
• _____ decision	Watching his older cousin run the Boston Marathon last April **influenced Tai's decision** to join the track team.
• strongly _____	The writer's personal life **strongly influenced** his novel.

Verbal Practice

Talk about It   **Read** each sentence and **think** about how you would complete it.

Discuss your idea with your partner using the sentence frame.

Listen carefully to your partner's and classmates' ideas.

Write your favorite idea in the blank.

❶ _____ **influenced** my plans last weekend.

❷ I think that _____ strongly **influences** a student's performance at school.

Writing Practice

Collaborate   **Work with your partner** to complete the sentence using the correct form of **influence** and appropriate content.

Some politicians use _____ to _____

people's decisions.

Your Turn   **Work independently** to complete the sentence using the correct form of **influence** and appropriate content.

_____ can _____ the behavior of young children.

Be an Academic Author   **Work independently** to write two sentences. In your first sentence, use **influence** in the *simple present tense* and include a word partner. In your second sentence, use **influence** in the *simple past tense*.

❶ _____

_____

❷ _____

_____

> **grammar tip**
>
> **To make the past simple tense of regular verbs, add –ed or –d.**
>
> Toni's ideas influenc**ed** my decision.
>
> Yesterday I play**ed** tennis.

Write an Academic Paragraph   **Complete** the paragraph using the correct form of **influence** and original content.

What would you do if you had the power to _____ a younger
           ❶

child's life? You already do have that _____ ! You may have younger
           ❷

_____ or cousins, or you may have friends with younger family
      ❸

members. Even if you don't, there are young people in your _____ who
           ❹

look up to teens like you as role models. If you want to positively _____
           ❺

a kid's life, you might consider volunteering for a mentoring program such as Teen Big

Brother or Big Sister. Or, if you are very good at a particular school subject or at sports, you

could be a _____ or an assistant coach. Think back to when you were
      ❻

_____ . How did older kids _____ you in a
      ❼   ❽

positive way?

integrate
verb

▶ **Say it:** in • te • grate   **Write it:** _____

<table>
<tr><th colspan="2">Meaning</th><th colspan="2">Example</th></tr>
<tr><td colspan="2">to bring different things or people together

Synonyms: combine, blend, unite, mix, incorporate</td><td colspan="2">Teachers try hard to **integrate** _____ into their _____ .</td></tr>
</table>

Forms		Family
Present:		• **Noun:** integration
I/You/We/They	integrate	• **Adjective:** integrated
He/She/It	integrates	
Past:	integrated	

Word Partners

- fully _____   This new software **fully integrates** five other programs.
- _____ (something, someone) into   When Lakeview High School closed, Jefferson High School **integrated** Lakeview's students **into** its classrooms.

Verbal Practice

Talk about It **Read** each sentence and **think** about how you would complete it.

Discuss your idea with your partner using the sentence frame.

Listen carefully to your partner's and classmates' ideas.

Write your favorite idea in the blank.

❶ You should **integrate** more _____ into your diet.

❷ New computer programs often **integrate** the features of

_____ .

Writing Practice

Collaborate   **Work with your partner** to complete the sentence using the correct form of **integrate** and appropriate content.

One way to help new students fully _____ into our school would be

to _____ .

Your Turn   **Work independently** to complete the sentence using the correct form of **integrate** and appropriate content.

It takes time and _____ to _____ new words into

your _____ .

Be an Academic Author   **Work independently** to write two sentences. In your first sentence, use **integrate** with the modal verb *should*. In your second sentence, use **integrate** with the adverb of frequency *often*. Include a word partner in one sentence.

❶ _____

_____

❷ _____

_____

> ### grammar tip
>
> Modal verbs are helping verbs that give additional meaning to the main verb. *Should* expresses advice.
>
> She **should integrate** more technology into the class.
>
> He **should study** harder.

Write an Academic Paragraph   **Complete** the paragraph using the correct form of **integrate** and original content.

More and more often, people are _____ their online
                                                        ❶

life with their offline life. Social media sites make this integration especially easy.

People can _____ their real-life friends and family into their
                                      ❷

_____ community and thus expand their communication
                 ❸

with them. While people are out and about in the real world, doing things

like _____ , eating in restaurants, or hanging out with
                 ❹

_____ , Web sites and applications like Facebook, Twitter, and Foursquare
               ❺

allow them to _____ where they are and what they are doing in an
                             ❻

online forum. In addition, smart phones have now _____ so many
                                                                   ❼

functions into one handheld device that people can do almost anything from anywhere.

interpret
verb

▶ **Say it:** in • **ter** • pret   *Write it:* _____

Academic Vocabulary Toolkit

Meanings	Examples
1. to change what someone is saying in one language to another language	1. Tran sometimes **interprets** for her _____ .
2. to decide on the meaning of something	2. I often **interpret** silence as _____ .

Forms	Family
Present: I/You/We/They interpret He/She/It interprets **Past:** interpreted	• **Noun:** interpretation, interpreter

Word Partners

- _____ the meaning of
- _____ the results

It can be difficult to **interpret the meaning of** some modern paintings.

Scientists have **interpreted the results** of the study to mean that the city will continue to grow.

Verbal Practice

Talk about It   **Read** each sentence and **think** about how you would complete it.

Discuss your idea with your partner using the sentence frame.

Listen carefully to your partner's and classmates' ideas.

Write your favorite idea in the blank.

❶ My cousin easily **interprets** Chinese into _____ .

❷ New immigrants sometimes need _____ to **interpret** for them.

❸ I usually **interpret** a smile to mean _____ .

❹ In English class, we sometimes **interpret** the meaning of a _____ .

Writing Practice

Collaborate **Work with your partner** to complete the sentence using the correct form of **interpret** and appropriate content.

Our science teacher has _____ the results of our tests to mean that

_____ .

Your Turn **Work independently** to complete the sentence using the correct form of **interpret** and appropriate content.

Before you get _____ , remember that there are many ways to

_____ the meaning of _____ .

Be an Academic Author **Work independently** to write two sentences using Meaning 2. In your first sentence, use **interpret** in the *simple present tense*. In your second sentence, use **interpret** in the *present perfect tense* and include a word partner.

❶ _____

_____

❷ _____

_____

> ### grammar tip
>
> The present perfect tense is formed with *has/have* + the past participle form of the verb. To make the past participle of regular verbs, add *–ed* or *–d*.
>
> He **has interpreted** the test results.
>
> She **has received** a letter.

Write an Academic Paragraph **Complete** the paragraph using the correct form of **interpret** and original content.

Teenagers and their parents often tend to _____ situations
❶

in different ways. Parents want their kids to be safe, to succeed in school and in life,

and to grow into responsible _____ . However, teenagers often
❷

_____ their parents' concerns as a desire to control them rather than
❸

as signs of love and protection. As a _____ , most teenagers try to
❹

rebel against the control of their parents. In turn, parents _____
❺

their kids' rebellion as disobedience, which leads to punishment. One solution to this

cycle of misunderstanding could be better_____ . If both sides are
❻

willing to _____ to the other, then there might be less room for
❼

misinterpretation.

interpretation
noun

▶ **Say it:** in • ter • pre • **ta** • tion   **Write it:** _____

Meaning	Example
an explanation or opinion about what something means **Synonym:** understanding	My friend and I had _____ different **interpretations** of the movie _____ .

Forms	Family
• **Singular:** interpretation • **Plural:** interpretations	• **Verb:** interpret • **Adjective:** interpreted

Word Partners	
• correct _____	The graph was so confusing it was hard to make a **correct interpretation** of the data.
• _____ of the results	I trust my doctor's **interpretation of the results** of the blood test.

Verbal Practice

Talk about It   **Read** each sentence and **think** about how you would complete it.

Discuss your idea with your partner using the sentence frame.

Listen carefully to your partner's and classmates' ideas.

Write your favorite idea in the blank.

❶ My friends and I disagree about the correct **interpretation** of

_____ .

❷ My **interpretation** of _____ is different from my mother's.

Writing Practice

Collaborate — **Work with your partner** to complete the sentence using the correct form of **interpretation** and appropriate content.

There are a variety of possible _____ of the results of the

_____ .

Your Turn — **Work independently** to complete the sentence using the correct form of **interpretation** and appropriate content.

In the story, which character is _____ and which one is _____

is open to _____ .

Be an Academic Author — **Work independently** to write two sentences. In your first sentence, use **interpretation** in the *singular form* and include a word partner. In your second sentence, use **interpretation** in the *plural form* with the quantifier *a variety of*.

❶ _____

_____

❷ _____

_____

> **grammar tip**
>
> Quantifiers are words that tell us how much or how many of a something there is. They usually come before the noun they are describing.
>
> This poem is open to **a variety of** interpretations.
>
> **A number of** students wear jeans every day.

Write an Academic Paragraph — **Complete** the paragraph using the correct form of **interpretation** and original content.

No matter how clearly written a law may be, there is always some room for

_____ . Legislators, who write and pass _____ ,
❶ ❷

cannot always imagine all of the ways that the law might affect people. If citizens do not

_____ a law, they can file a _____ . Judges
❸ ❹

listen to the case and decide whether the law is _____ . Some cases
❺

may go all the way to the Supreme Court. When the nine justices of the Supreme Court

vote, the ruling of the _____ becomes the official court ruling.
❻

Once the Supreme Court interprets a law, the lower courts must follow the Supreme Court's

_____ .
❼

103

investigate
verb

Say it: in • **ves** • ti • gate   **Write it:** _____

Meaning	Example
to try and find out information about something **Synonyms:** look into, research, examine	We heard a noise coming from the _____ last night, so my _____ went down to **investigate**.

Forms		Family
Present: I/You/We/They He/She/It	investigate investigates	• **Nouns:** investigation, investigator • **Adjective:** investigative
Past:	investigated	

Word Partners

• fully _____	Before you buy a used car, you should **fully investigate** its history online.
• _____ further	For your report, choose a topic that you find interesting and want to **investigate further**.
• _____ the possibility of	Scientists have **investigated the possibility of** life on other planets.

Verbal Practice

Talk about It **Read** each sentence and **think** about how you would complete it.

Discuss your idea with your partner using the sentence frame.

Listen carefully to your partner's and classmates' ideas.

Write your favorite idea in the blank.

❶ When I heard that _____ , I had to **investigate** further.

❷ In some cases, _____ are used to **investigate** a crime.

104

Writing Practice

Collaborate **Work with your partner** to complete the sentence using the correct form of **investigate** and appropriate content.

Our school should fully _____ the possibility of offering _____

and _____ to students.

Your Turn **Work independently** to complete the sentence using the correct form of **investigate** and appropriate content.

Scientists _____ natural disasters, such as _____ and

_____ , in order to learn how to predict when they will happen.

Be an Academic Author **Work independently** to write two sentences. In your first sentence, use **investigate** in the *simple present tense*. In your second sentence, use **investigate** with the modal verb *should* and include a word partner.

❶ _____

_____

❷ _____

_____

> ### grammar tip
>
> Modal verbs are helping verbs that give additional meaning to the main verb. *Should* expresses advice.
>
> You **should** investigate other careers.
>
> Alex **should** stop talking in class.

Write an Academic Paragraph **Complete** the paragraph using the correct form of **investigate** and original content.

It's never too soon to start thinking about what career you might want. Now is a good

time for you to start to _____ all of the possibilities. If you like
                              ❶

technology, software development or _____ are areas you
                                        ❷

should consider. Do you like biology? Perhaps you could become a scientific researcher,

who _____ cures for diseases. If you're good with languages,
        ❸

you could be a _____ or work for an international company.
                    ❹

Perhaps you are a creative person. You could be a graphic designer, a musician, or a

_____ . Start by _____ a list of all of your
        ❺   ❻

interests. Then go _____ to a career-building Web site or a job-hunting
                        ❼

site to see what's out there.

maintain
verb

▶ **Say it:** main • **tain**   *Write it:* _____

Academic Vocabulary Toolkit

Meanings	Examples
1. to keep something in good condition **Synonyms:** take care of, keep up	**1.** Change the _____ every 3,000 miles to **maintain** your car's engine.
2. to say something is true **Synonyms:** believe, declare	**2.** The _____ of both pizza places **maintain** that they have the best _____ .

Forms	Family
Present: I/You/We/They maintain He/She/It maintains **Past:** maintained	• **Noun:** maintenance

Word Partners

- ____ a balance   She **maintains a balance** of work and fun in her life.
- ____ order   The army **maintained order** after the riots.
- struggle to ____   The company **struggles to maintain** quality as it grows rapidly.

Verbal Practice

Talk about It **Read** each sentence and **think** about how you would complete it.

Discuss your idea with your partner using the sentence frame.

Listen carefully to your partner's and classmates' ideas.

Write your favorite idea in the blank.

❶ If you want to _____ , it's important to **maintain** good grades.

❷ Some people struggle to **maintain** their _____ .

❸ Most teachers **maintain** that homework helps students to

_____ .

❹ The owner of the fast-food restaurant **maintained** that the food there is

_____ .

Writing Practice

Collaborate **Work with your partner** to complete the sentences using the correct form of **maintain** and appropriate content.

❶ It is the responsibility of _____ to _____ order on the bus.

❷ I have always _____ that _____ is the best _____ player ever.

Your Turn **Work independently** to complete the sentences using the correct form of **maintain** and appropriate content.

❶ I find it difficult to _____ a balance between _____ and _____ .

❷ In my article, I _____ that teachers should _____ .

Be an Academic Author **Work independently** to write two sentences. In your first sentence, use **maintain** in the *simple past tense* and include a word partner. In your second sentence, use **maintain** in the *present perfect tense*.

MEANING ❶ _____
_____

MEANING ❷ _____
_____

> ### grammar tip
>
> The present perfect tense is formed with *has/have* + the past participle form of the verb. To make the past participle of regular verbs, add *−ed* or *−d*.
>
> She **has** maintain**ed** her home very well.
>
> They **have** received As in all their classes.

Write an Academic Paragraph **Complete** the paragraph using the correct form of **maintain** and original content.

Most students are excited at the beginning of a new school year.

They go shopping for new _____ and _____ .
　　　　　　　　　　　　　　　　❶　　　　　　　　　　　　　　　❷

They promise to _____ a balance between school and socializing.
　　　　　　　　　　❸

However, maintaining this _____ isn't always easy. Often, by
　　　　　　　　　　　　　　　❹

_____ , most students have slipped back into their old routine. They
　　　❺

find themselves _____ when they should be studying. How can
　　　　　　　　　❻

students _____ their motivation for school? Try looking ahead. View
　　　　　　❼

every day as a step toward a _____ future.
　　　　　　　　　　　　　　　❽

modify
verb

Say it: **mod** · i · fy

Write it: _____

Academic Vocabulary Toolkit

Meaning	Example
to change something in a small way *Synonyms:* alter, change	Antonio **modified** his _____ so that it would run on used _____ oil.

Forms		Family
Present: I/You/We/They modify He/She/It modifies *Past:* modified		• **Noun:** modification • **Adjective:** modified

Word Partners

- _____ (my/your/his/her/their/our) behavior
- _____ the rules

Huan **modified his behavior** and is now more respectful to adults.

The game was too difficult for five-year-olds, so they **modified the rules** slightly.

Verbal Practice

Talk about It   **Read** each sentence and **think** about how you would complete it.

     Discuss your idea with your partner using the sentence frame.

     Listen carefully to your partner's and classmates' ideas.

     Write your favorite idea in the blank.

❶ Dog trainers can **modify** a dog's behavior by rewarding good behavior with

_____ .

❷ Teachers sometimes **modify** their lesson plan to

_____ .

Writing Practice

Collaborate   **Work with your partner** to complete the sentence using the correct form of **modify** and appropriate content.

I _____ my after-school routine by spending less time _____ .

Your Turn   **Work independently** to complete the sentence using the correct form of **modify** and appropriate content.

I like the new version of the game because they added new _____ and

_____ the rules to make it _____ to win.

Be an Academic Author   **Work independently** to write two sentences. In your first sentence, use **modify** with a word partner. In your second sentence, use **modify** with the adverb of frequency *sometimes*.

❶ _____

_____

❷ _____

_____

> ### grammar tip
>
> Adverbs of frequency tell how often something happens. They usually go before the main verb.
>
> He <u>sometimes</u> modifies his routine by driving instead of walking.

Write an Academic Paragraph   **Complete** the paragraph using the correct form of **modify** and original content.

Your parents, your teachers, and even the U.S. _____ ❶ want you to eat

healthier food. Since kids tend to choose _____ ❷ food even when they

have healthy choices, the government funded research on how to _____ ❸

kids' eating habits. The researchers found that kids change what they eat when school cafeterias

_____ ❹ the way they display food. Putting the salad bar by the register and

placing _____ ❺ milk behind regular milk were two ideas. Students also

_____ ❻ their habits when the cafeteria displayed fruit in colorful bowls and

accepted only cash for dessert items like _____ ❼ . Perhaps small changes

such as these will help students permanently _____ ❽ their eating habits.

obtain
verb

Say it: ob • **tain**   Write it: _____

Academic Vocabulary Toolkit

Meaning	Example
to get something, usually after some effort	After playing the game for _____ hours, John **obtained** the _____ score.

Forms	Family
Present: I/You/We/They obtain He/She/It obtains **Past:** obtained	• *Adjective:* obtainable

Word Partners

- able to _____   Gina was **able to obtain** a U.S. passport when she became a citizen.
- difficult to _____   It's **difficult to obtain** an A in Mrs. Nero's class.
- _____ permission   The producers **obtained permission** from the town to film the movie at night.

Verbal Practice

Talk about It   **Read** each sentence and **think** about how you would complete it.

Discuss your idea with your partner using the sentence frame.

Listen carefully to your partner's and classmates' ideas.

Write your favorite idea in the blank.

❶ You should be able to **obtain** a copy of your _____ online.

❷ Before you travel to a foreign country, you must **obtain** a _____ .

Writing Practice

Collaborate **Work with your partner** to complete the sentences using the correct form of **obtain** and appropriate content.

After asking many times, I finally _____ permission from my parents to

_____ .

Your Turn **Work independently** to complete the sentences using the correct form of **obtain** and appropriate content.

If you don't have a job, it will be difficult to _____ a _____ .

Be an Academic Author **Work independently** to write two sentences. In your first sentence, use **obtain** in the *simple past tense* and include the word partner *obtain permission*. In your second sentence, use **obtain** with the modal verb *must*.

❶ _____

_____

❷ _____

_____

> **grammar tip**
>
> **Modal verbs are helping verbs that give additional meaning to the main verb.** *Must* **expresses necessity.**
>
> You **must obtain** permission to go on the trip.
>
> Raul **must stop** talking in class.

Write an Academic Paragraph **Complete** the paragraph using the correct form of **obtain** and original content.

Fans often ask celebrities such as _____ if they can take their picture
❶

or have their autograph. Obtaining _____ or photos with a star
❷

can be fun. However, sometimes the public's obsession with _____
❸

can go too far. Paparazzi are photographers who take photos for magazines. Often, they

don't _____ permission before they take pictures of a star. Instead,
❹

they follow celebrities in cars and into stores, and even _____ !
❺

Paparazzi _____ information about stars from their house cleaners,
❻

their children's teachers, and even from looking through their _____ .
❼

It must be very exciting to be a celebrity, but it is hard to keep your life private.

occur
verb

Write it: _____

Academic Vocabulary Toolkit

Meaning	Example
to happen, especially without planning **Synonyms:** happen, come about	When _____ and other natural disasters **occur**, _____ report on the events.

Forms	Family
Present: I/You/We/They occur He/She/It occurs **Past:** occurred	• **Noun:** occurrence

Word Partners

• event _____	What important **event occurred** in 1776?
• likely to _____	Car accidents are very **likely to occur** at night.
• frequently _____	The color green **frequently occurs** in nature; leaves, grass, and flower stems are some examples.

Verbal Practice

Talk about It   **Read** each sentence and **think** about how you would complete it.

Discuss your idea with your partner using the sentence frame.

Listen carefully to your partner's and classmates' ideas.

Write your favorite idea in the blank.

❶ The most dangerous room in the house is the _____ ; that's where accidents are most likely to **occur**.

❷ Problems between family members frequently **occur** when _____ .

Writing Practice

Collaborate   Work with your partner to complete the sentences using the correct form of **occur** and appropriate content.

Last year, an event _____ in _____ that will change the

world forever.

Your Turn   Work independently to complete the sentences using the correct form of **occur** and appropriate content.

Two names that frequently _____ at our school are _____

and _____ .

Be an Academic Author   Work independently to write two sentences. In your first sentence, use **occur** in the *simple past tense* with the word partner *frequently occur*. In your second sentence, use **occur** in the *simple present tense*.

❶ _____

_____

❷ _____

_____

> **grammar tip**
>
> Some verbs that end in a consonant-vowel-consonant form their past tense by doubling the final consonant and adding –*ed*.
>
> Many accidents occur**red** during the storm.
>
> The mayor permit**ted** workers to leave early.

Write an Academic Paragraph   Complete the paragraph using the correct form of **occur** and original content.

Each month, Earth's moon passes through several stages, or phases.

The phases of the _____❶ are named for how much of the moon we

can see. The new moon phase _____❷ when the moon is between the

Earth and the sun. The back of the moon is lit by the _____❸ . We can't

see that part of the moon on Earth, so the moon looks _____❹ to us.

A full moon _____❺ when the moon is on the opposite side of the Earth.

The part of the moon that is lit by the sun faces _____❻ . We can see the

entire face of the moon. During the half-moon phase, we see half of the moon, but the other

_____❼ is in shadow.

113

opponent

noun

Say it: op • **po** • nent   **Write it:** _____

Academic Vocabulary Toolkit

Meaning	Example	
a person who is on the opposite side in a fight, game, debate, or contest **Synonyms:** competitor, rival	The _____ went wild when the home _____ beat their **opponents**.	**GO RAVENS!** HOME 87 00:00 VISITOR 83 PERIOD 4 BONUS BONUS FOULS PLAYER FOULS FOULS GAME

Forms	Family
• *Singular:* opponent • *Plural:* opponents	• *Noun:* opposition • *Adjective:* opposite, opposing

Word Partners	
• worthy _____	My brother is a **worthy opponent** in a chess match; he's very smart!
• political _____	The two **political opponents** will face each other in the November election.

Verbal Practice

Talk about It **Read** each sentence and **think** about how you would complete it.

Discuss your idea with your partner using the sentence frame.

Listen carefully to your partner's and classmates' ideas.

Write your favorite idea in the blank.

❶ When you play _____ , you want to

_____ before your **opponent** does.

❷ Our _____ team plays against some worthy **opponents**,

such as _____ .

Writing Practice

Collaborate **Work with your partner** to complete the sentence using the correct form of **opponent** and appropriate content.

The president and the _____ are _____ , but on

Sundays they _____ .

Your Turn **Work independently** to complete the sentence using the correct form of **opponent** and appropriate content.

_____ of a political party or a government sometimes voice their opinion

by _____ .

Be an Academic Author **Work independently** to write two sentences. In your first sentence, use **opponent** in the *singular form* and include a word partner. In your second sentence, use **opponent** in the *plural form*.

❶ _____

_____

❷ _____

_____

> ### grammar tip
>
> Count nouns name things that can be counted. Count nouns have two forms, singular and plural. To make most count nouns plural, add –*s*.
>
> The boxing champion has faced many opponent**s**.
>
> Ethan likes board games.

Write an Academic Paragraph **Complete** the paragraph using the correct form of **opponent** and original content.

Today, schools in the United States are integrated. Every school must allow students of

every _____ or ethnicity to attend. However, before the Civil Rights
             ❶

Movement of the 1960s, many _____ , especially in the South,
                                    ❷

were segregated. There were _____ schools for white students
                                 ❸

and African-American students. _____ of segregation protested
                                    ❹

to show the government that _____ was wrong. They voiced their
                                 ❺

opposition in marches and boycotts. They faced violence and even death at the hands

of their _____ . When the first schools were integrated, young
              ❻

African-American students had to be very courageous. These children paved the way for the

_____ .
       ❼

oppose
verb

▶ **Say it:** op • **pose**   ***Write it:*** _____

Meaning	Example
to be against someone or something *Synonym:* disagree with	In the 1800s, abolitionists like Frederick Douglass strongly **opposed** _____ .

Forms	Family
Present: I/You/We/They oppose He/She/It opposes ***Past:*** opposed	• ***Nouns:*** opposition, opponent • ***Adjectives:*** opposing, opposed, opposite

Word Partners
• strongly _____   I **strongly oppose** all forms of racism and sexism.

Verbal Practice

Talk about It   **Read** each sentence and **think** about how you would complete it.

                Discuss your idea with your partner using the sentence frame.

                Listen carefully to your partner's and classmates' ideas.

                Write your favorite idea in the blank.

❶ What kind of person **opposes** a law that _____ ?

❷ My father was strongly **opposed** to my plan to _____ .

116

Writing Practice

Collaborate | **Work with your partner** to complete the sentence using the correct form of **oppose** and appropriate content.

If you _____ cruelty to animals, then you should _____ .

Your Turn | **Work independently** to complete the sentence using the correct form of **oppose** and appropriate content.

I would never _____ a suggestion to _____ .

Be an Academic Author | **Work independently** to write two sentences. In your first sentence, use **oppose** with the adverb of frequency *never*. In your second sentence, use **oppose** in the *present tense* and include the word partner *strongly oppose*.

❶ _____

_____

❷ _____

_____

> ### grammar tip
>
> Adverbs of frequency are words that tell how often something happens. They usually go before the main verb.
>
> He **never** opposes his father's wishes.
>
> She **frequently** arrives late.

Write an Academic Paragraph | **Complete** the paragraph using the correct form of **oppose** and original content.

Imagine that your school district suggested extending the school year through the

_____ . Would you support or _____ this
      ❶   ❷

plan? Under this new plan, summer vacations would be four to six weeks long. Winter

and _____ vacations would be two or three weeks. Would you still
        ❸

_____ the plan? Supporters say this plan would increase student
      ❹

_____ . During the traditional long summer vacation, many students
      ❺

_____ much of what they learned the year before. The first few
      ❻

weeks of every school year are spent _____ . A longer school year
                               ❼

gives teachers more time to teach new material.

opposition
noun

Say it: op • po • **si** • tion   **Write it:** _____

<table>
<tr><td rowspan="5">Academic Vocabulary Toolkit</td><td>Meaning</td><td colspan="2">Example</td></tr>
<tr><td>strong disagreement

Synonyms: disagreement, protest</td><td>The developer's plan to cut down _____ to build a _____ met with opposition.</td><td></td></tr>
<tr><td colspan="3">Family</td></tr>
<tr><td colspan="3">• Verb: oppose
• Adjective: opposing, opposed, opposite</td></tr>
<tr><td colspan="3">Word Partners</td></tr>
</table>

- express (my/your/his/her/our/their) _____   The groups **expressed their opposition** to the capture of dolphins.
- face _____   The president's plan **faces opposition** from Congress.
- strong _____   There is **strong opposition** in my neighborhood to the plan to build a car wash.

Verbal Practice

Talk about It   **Read** each sentence and **think** about how you would complete it.

   Discuss your idea with your partner using the sentence frame.

   Listen carefully to your partner's and classmates' ideas.

   Write your favorite idea in the blank.

❶ I would face **opposition** at home if I tried to _____ .

❷ If our teacher _____ , there would be strong **opposition** from students.

Writing Practice

Collaborate — **Work with your partner** to complete the sentence using **opposition** and appropriate content.

Many nations joined together to express their _____ to _____ .

Your Turn — **Work independently** to complete the sentence using **opposition** and appropriate content.

Anyone who tried to _____ in our neighborhood would face

tremendous _____ .

Be an Academic Author — **Work independently** to write two sentences. In your first sentence, use **opposition** with the word partner *face opposition*. In your second sentence, use **opposition** with another word partner.

❶ _____

_____

❷ _____

_____

> **grammar tip**
>
> **Non-count nouns name things that can't be counted. Non-count nouns have only one form. Do not add an −s to a non-count noun.**
>
> The new leaders faced **opposition** to their plans.
>
> The **water** in the river is frozen.

Write an Academic Paragraph — **Complete** the paragraph using **opposition** and original content.

When you disagree with a government or school policy, how do

you voice your _____ ❶ ? One common way for people to express

their _____ ❷ to something is to complain about it to their friends.

However, this has very little _____ ❸ on the policy! A more effective

_____ ❹ would be to start a petition, collecting the names and

_____ ❺ of people who share your opinions. Then deliver the petition to

_____ ❻ in a position to change the policy. Or, you could start a Twitter

campaign. Create a Twitter account and send _____ ❼ for friends to

forward. There are many ways to voice your opposition other than simply grumbling!

option
noun

Say it: **op** • tion   **Write it:** _____

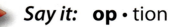

Academic Vocabulary Toolkit

Meaning	Example
a choice between two or more things	At a _____ American supermarket, you always have _____ of **options** to choose from, no matter what you are looking for.

Forms	Family
• *Singular:* option • *Plural:* options	• *Verb:* opt • *Adjective:* optional

Word Partners	
• consider (my/your/his/her/their/our) _____ s	After receiving three job offers, Wendy **considered her options,** thinking over the good and bad points of each position.
• given the _____	When **given the option** of ice cream or cake, I will always choose ice cream.

Verbal Practice

Talk about It   **Read** each sentence and **think** about how you would complete it.

Discuss your idea with your partner using the sentence frame.

Listen carefully to your partner's and classmates' ideas.

Write your favorite idea in the blank.

❶ Given the **option**, I would rather communicate with people

_____ .

❷ If I had the **option** of visiting any place in the world right now, I would go to

_____ .

Writing Practice

Collaborate **Work with your partner** to complete the sentence using the correct form of **option** and appropriate content.

Given the _____ of eating _____ or _____ for

lunch, I would choose _____ .

Your Turn **Work independently** to complete the sentence using the correct form of **option** and appropriate content.

When I have to make a big decision, I consider my _____ and then

I _____ .

Be an Academic Author **Work independently** to write two sentences. In your first sentence, use **option** in the *singular form* and include the word partner *given the option*. In your second sentence, use **option** in the *plural form*.

❶ _____

_____

❷ _____

_____

> **grammar tip**
>
> **Count nouns name things that can be counted. Count nouns have two forms, singular and plural. To make most count nouns plural, add –s.**
>
> Consider all your option**s** before deciding.
>
> He likes board game**s**.

Write an Academic Paragraph **Complete** the paragraph using the correct form of **option** and original content.

Is it better to have too many _____ rather
❶

than too few? In fact, having too many _____ can be overwhelming.
❷

Haven't you ever stood in an aisle of a _____ staring at all the products
❸

available, unable to decide which was the best? But this issue also affects larger decisions. What

college should I go to? What should I study? What career should I _____ ?
❹

Now with the Internet, the whole _____ is open to us. Many of us are
❺

more confused than ever! Some studies have shown that children who are given very limited

_____ tend to be more successful in their chosen activities than
❻

children who are given unlimited _____ . Do our unlimited choices limit
❼

our success?

organization
noun

▶ **Say it:** or • ga • ni • **za** • tion   **Write it:** _____

Meanings	Examples	
1. a group of people working together with a common purpose **Synonyms:** institution, company, club, group	**1.** The _____ is an **organization** that helps people.	
2. the way in which something is arranged **Synonyms:** neatness, order, grouping **Antonym:** disorganization	**2.** I was _____ by the **organization** of Jasmine's _____ .	

Forms	Family
• **Singular:** organization • **Plural:** organizations	• **Verb:** organize • **Adjective:** organized, organizational

Word Partners	
• lack of _____	The speaker's **lack of organization** made it hard to follow his argument.
• improve the _____	Making an outline will **improve the organization** of your essays.

Verbal Practice

Talk about It   **Read** each frame and **think** about how you would complete it.

Discuss your idea with your partner using the sentence frame.

Listen carefully to your partner's and classmates' ideas.

Write your favorite idea in the blank.

❶ An example of a student **organization** is _____ .

❷ _____ is an **organization** that helps animals.

❸ A lack of **organization** could cause you to _____ .

❹ The **organization** of items in _____ helps people find them easily.

Writing Practice

Collaborate **Work with your partner** to complete the sentence using **organization** and appropriate content.

When we write reports, our teacher grades us on the _____ of our ideas as

well as on our grammar and _____ .

Your Turn **Work independently** to complete the sentence using **organization** and appropriate content.

Maybe if I improved my _____ and time management skills, I would

_____ .

Be an Academic Author **Work independently** to write two sentences using Meaning 2 of **organization**. In your first sentence, use **organization** with the word partner *improve the organization*. In your second sentence, use **organization** with the word partner *lack of organization*.

❶ _____

_____

❷ _____

_____

> ### grammar tip
>
> **Non-count nouns are nouns that can't be counted. Non-count nouns have only one form. Do not add an −s to a non-count noun. Meaning 2 of *organization* is a non-count noun.**
>
> Your essay lacks **organization**.

Write an Academic Paragraph **Complete** the paragraph using **organization** and original content.

Everyone misplaces a book or _____ once in a while.
❶

However, if you find that a lack of _____ is hurting your grades
❷

and affecting other areas of your life, it might be time to do something. What can you do to

improve your organizational _____ ? Many formerly disorganized
❸

students say that using a planner is a _____ . A planner can be
❹

_____ or just a simple notebook. The important thing is to use it. In your
❺

planner, write down all your homework assignments, _____ , meetings,
❻

and study times. Use your planner every day to add _____ to your life.
❼

organize
verb

▶ **Say it:** or • ga • nize   **Write it:** _____

Meaning	Example
to put things in order	It's much easier to find the things you _____
Synonyms: arrange, order	if you **organize** your
Antonym: disorganize	_____ .

Forms		Family
Present:		• *Nouns:* organization, organizer
I/You/We/They	organize	• *Adjective:* organized, organizational
He/She/It	organizes	
Past:	organized	

Word Partners	
• help _____	Technology can **help organize** your life.
• able to _____	I am **able to organize** all my photos on one Web site.

Verbal Practice

Talk about It **Read** each sentence and **think** about how you would complete it.

Discuss your idea with your partner using the sentence frame.

Listen carefully to your partner's and classmates' ideas.

Write your favorite idea in the blank.

❶ I'm writing an outline to help **organize** my _____ .

❷ The coach is **organizing** a _____ tournament.

Writing Practice

Collaborate **Work with your partner** to complete the sentence using the correct form of **organize** and appropriate content.

The library _____ books according to _____ and

_____ .

Your Turn **Work independently** to complete the sentence using the correct form of **organize** and appropriate content.

Last year, students at our school were able to _____ a _____ .

Be an Academic Author **Work independently** to write two sentences. In your first sentence, use **organize** in the *simple present tense*. In your second sentence, use **organize** in the *present progressive tense*.

❶ _____

_____

❷ _____

_____

> **grammar tip**
>
> **The present progressive tense is formed with *am/is/are* and a verb ending in *–ing*.**
>
> Today I **am organizing** my desk.
>
> She **is running** down the street.

Write an Academic Paragraph **Complete** the paragraph using the correct form of **organize** and original content.

Some people, mostly teenagers, say that a _____❶_____ and

disorganized room is a sign of genius. Others, mostly mothers, say it is just a sign of being a

_____❷_____ . No matter what you believe, there comes a time when even

the most brilliant _____❸_____ needs to clean up his or her room and get

_____❹_____ . Here are some hints to help all of you geniuses get started.

Begin by throwing away or donating anything that you don't _____❺_____

anymore. Then, _____❻_____ items into categories: books, clothes, school

supplies, electronics, and so on. Store all similar items _____❼_____ . This

could be your first step toward a more organized life.

participate
verb

▶ **Say it:** par • **tic** • i • pate   **Write it:** _____

Meaning	Example
to have a role in an activity or an event	Candidates for class _____ agreed to **participate** in a _____ on Tuesday.
Synonym: take part	

Forms		Family
Present:		• *Nouns:* participation, participant
I/You/We/They	participate	• *Adjective:* participatory
He/She/It	participates	
Past:	participated	

Word Partners	
• actively _____	Citizens should **actively participate** in the democratic process.
• agree to_____	Many sets of twins **agreed to participate** in a research study.

Verbal Practice

Talk about It   **Read** each sentence and **think** about how you would complete it.

Discuss your idea with your partner using the sentence frame.

Listen carefully to your partner's and classmates' ideas.

Write your favorite idea in the blank.

❶ In the reality show _____ , the audience can actively

participate by voting for their favorite _____ .

❷ I would encourage other students to **participate** in _____ .

Writing Practice

Collaborate **Work with your partner** to complete the sentence using the correct form of **participate** and appropriate content.

The peace talks were a success because _____ agreed to

_____ .

Your Turn **Work independently** to complete the sentence using the correct form of **participate** and appropriate content.

Last year when I _____ in _____ , I had to prepare

by _____ .

Be an Academic Author **Work independently** to write two sentences. In your first sentence, use **participate** in the *simple past tense*. In your second sentence, use **participate** with a word partner.

1 _____

_____

2 _____

_____

> ### grammar tip
>
> **To make the simple past tense of regular verbs, add –ed or –d.**
>
> She participat**ed** in the chess tournament.
>
> I play**ed** tennis yesterday.

Write an Academic Paragraph **Complete** the paragraph using the correct form of **participate** and original content.

Many students _____ in extracurricular activities after the
1

regular school day is done. Extracurricular activities are optional; you don't have to

_____ if you don't want to. However, many students find that
2

participation in these _____ is fun, and you can learn a lot. If you sign up
3

for a _____ , or to organize a school dance, you have made a commitment
4

to be a part of a group. Being a participant can teach you to cooperate with others and to be

_____ . Other students are _____ on you. For
5   **6**

example, if you are on the _____ team, and you don't show up to a
7

game, the team might not win. Extracurricular _____ teach valuable
8

lessons to students; your education can continue, even after the school bell rings!

pattern
noun

▶ **Say it:** pat · tern   **Write it:** _____

Academic Vocabulary Toolkit

Meanings	Examples
1. a design of regular shapes, lines, or colors	1. Mike and May couldn't agree on a **pattern** for the _____ .
2. a repeated set of events, characteristics, or features	2. January 1 is a good time to _____ your usual **patterns** of _____ .

1. Eat more vegetables
2. Study harder
3. Practice piano
4. Be nicer to brothers

Forms	Family
• **Singular:** pattern • **Plural:** patterns	• **Verb:** pattern • **Adjective:** patterned

Word Partners

• follow a _____	Every school year, Najan's actions **follow a pattern**; at first, he does very well, but by the second week of school, he starts clowning around.
• _____ of behavior	Frequent lying is a **pattern of behavior** that worries me.

Verbal Practice

Talk about It **Read** each sentence and **think** about how you would complete it.

Discuss your idea with your partner using the sentence frame.

Listen carefully to your partner's and classmates' ideas.

Write your favorite idea in the blank.

❶ Many bathing suits have colorful **patterns**, such as _____ .

❷ The artist used a **pattern** of _____ and _____ in her painting.

❸ Academic essays usually follow a **pattern**; they begin with an _____ and end with a conclusion.

❹ Most _____ follow similar **patterns**.

128

Writing Practice

Collaborate **Work with your partner** to complete the sentence using the correct form of **pattern** and appropriate content.

_____ usually have predictable _____ of behavior.

Your Turn **Work independently** to complete the sentence using the correct form of **pattern** and appropriate content.

My morning routine usually follows the same _____ every school day; first

I _____ and then I _____ .

Be an Academic Author **Work independently** to write two sentences using Meaning 2. In your first sentence, use **pattern** in the *singular form* and include a word partner. In your second sentence, use **pattern** in the *plural form*.

❶ _____

_____

❷ _____

_____

grammar tip

Count nouns name things that can be counted. Count nouns have two forms, singular and plural. To make most count nouns plural, add *-s*.

Patterns of behavior can be hard to change.

He likes board games.

Write an Academic Paragraph **Complete** the paragraph using the correct form of **pattern** and original content.

Every child is unique, but most babies follow a _____ pattern of
                                                                                ❶

development. New parents need to understand the _____ and physical
                                                                         ❷

growth _____ of babies. During their first two years of life, babies grow
              ❸

rapidly. As they grow, their _____ skills improve. They first learn to sit up,
                                          ❹

then crawl, and then stand up; then, sometime between 11 and 18 months, most children will start

to _____ . At the same time that they are growing physically, children
          ❺

are also _____ emotionally. From their parents, they are learning how to
                ❻

trust and to how to show _____ . Although they are still tiny, children are
                                        ❼

developing _____ of behavior that they will carry with them for the rest
                  ❽

of their lives.

perceive
verb

▶ **Say it:** per • ceive   **Write it:** _____

Meaning	Example
to understand or think about something in a certain way **Synonyms:** know, grasp	Students who **perceive** themselves as _____ are more likely to be _____ .

Forms		Family
Present: I/You/We/They perceive He/She/It perceives **Past:** perceived		• **Noun:** perception • **Adjective:** perceptive, perceptible • **Adverb:** perceivably, perceptively

Word Partners	
• _____ (something) differently	Do you think women **perceive** the world **differently** than men?
• _____ themselves	Few people **perceive themselves** as dishonest.

Verbal Practice

Talk about It   **Read** each sentence and **think** about how you would complete it.

         Discuss your idea with your partner using the sentence frame.

         Listen carefully to your partner's and classmates' ideas.

         Write your favorite idea in the blank.

❶ My friends see me as a _____ , but I **perceive** myself differently.

❷ All the members of the _____ **perceived** one another as equals.

Writing Practice

Collaborate **Work with your partner** to complete the sentence using the correct form of **perceive** and appropriate content.

Sugar is often _____ to be the cause of _____ .

Your Turn **Work independently** to complete the sentences using the correct form of **perceive** and appropriate content.

Some people _____ themselves as _____ than they are.

Be an Academic Author **Work independently** to write two sentences. In your first sentence, use **perceive** in the *simple present tense* with a person's name. In your second sentence, use **perceive** in the *simple past tense* and include the word partner *perceive themselves*.

❶ _____

_____

❷ _____

_____

> ### grammar tip
> In the simple present tense, the third person (*he, she, it*) form takes an *–s* or *–es* ending.
>
> She perceiv**es** everyone to be her enemy.
>
> Mr. Tom teach**es** my biology class.

Write an Academic Paragraph **Complete** the paragraph using the correct form of **perceive** and original content.

You may not be able to change the world, but you can change the way you

_____ it. Imagine that you are planning to go hiking or play
❶

_____ outside with your friends. Just as you are about to leave, it starts
❷

to rain. You can't stop the rain, but you can change how you _____
❸

the rain. Maybe the rain is good, because now you and your friends can watch the

_____ you wanted to see. The same is true for bigger issues.
❹

For example, if you perceive _____ to a new town as scary, it
❺

will be _____ . However, if you _____
❻ ❼

moving as exciting, it will be exciting. You will meet new people and have new

_____ . Changing your perceptions can turn a negative situation into
❽

a positive one.

perception
noun

<table>
<tr><td colspan="2">

Academic Vocabulary Toolkit

</td></tr>
</table>

Academic Vocabulary Toolkit

Meaning	Example
the way that someone thinks about something **Synonyms:** idea, understanding, belief **Antonym:** misperception	Many _____ have the **perception** that expensive brands are _____ .

Forms	Family
• **Singular:** perception • **Plural:** perceptions	• **Adjective:** perceptive • **Adverb:** perceptively • **Verb:** perceive

Word Partners	
• change (my/his/her/your/their/our) _____	Smell can **change our perception** of how food tastes.
• negative _____	Many people have a **negative perception** of homeless people.

Verbal Practice

Talk about It   **Read** each sentence and **think** about how you would complete it.

Discuss your idea with your partner using the sentence frame.

Listen carefully to your partner's and classmates' ideas.

Write your favorite idea in the blank.

❶ Some people have a negative **perception** of lawyers because they think they

_____ .

❷ Teenagers often have the **perception** that older people _____ .

Writing Practice

Collaborate　**Work with your partner** to complete the sentences using the correct form of **perception** and appropriate content.

Newspapers and _____ shape our _____ of

_____ .

Your Turn　**Work independently** to complete the sentences using the correct form of **perception** and appropriate content.

Older people often have negative _____ of young people who

_____ .

Be an Academic Author　**Work independently** to write two sentences. In your first sentence, use **perception** in the *singular form* and include a word partner. In your second sentence, use **perception** in the *plural form*.

❶ _____

_____

❷ _____

_____

> ### grammar tip
>
> **Count nouns name things that can be counted. Count nouns have two forms, singular and plural. To make most count nouns plural, add –s.**
>
> People's perception**s** of the war changed.
>
> He likes board game**s**.

Write an Academic Paragraph　**Complete** the paragraph using the correct form of **perception** and original content.

　　When a person is caught doing something wrong in our society,

punishment is the usual response. The punishment for a child who hits another child is usually

_____ . An adult caught robbing a _____ ,
　　　　　　　　❶　　　　　　　　　　　　　　　　　　　　　　　　❷

is sent to prison. Our society's _____ is that punishment is effective
　　　　　　　　　　　　　　　　❸

because it prevents people from doing _____ . However, in Africa there
　　　　　　　　　　　　　　　　　　　❹

is a tribe where the _____ is different. In this tribe, when someone
　　　　　　　　　❺

does something wrong, the community forms a circle around the wrongdoer. People talk

about all of the good things that person has done. Through this ceremony, people can change

their _____ of themselves. They remember that they are an important,
　　　❻

positive part of their _____ .
　　　　　　　　　　　❼

133

permit
verb

▶ **Say it:** per • **mit**   **Write it:** _____

Meaning	Example	
to allow	The _____ does not **permit** _____ in some areas.	NO CELL PHONE ZONE

Forms		Family
Present:		• **Nouns:** permit, permission
I/You/We/They	permit	• **Adjective:** permissible, permissive
He/She/It	permits	
Past:	permitted	

Verbal Practice

Talk about It   **Read** each sentence and **think** about how you would complete it.

Discuss your idea with your partner using the sentence frame.

Listen carefully to your partner's and classmates' ideas.

Write your favorite idea in the blank.

❶ Our English teacher sometimes **permits** students to _____ .

❷ One thing that my parents would never **permit** me to do is to

_____ .

Writing Practice

Collaborate   **Work with your partner** to complete the sentence using the correct form of **permit** and appropriate content.

Football rules _____ players to _____ .

Your Turn   **Work independently** to complete the sentence using the correct form of **permit** and appropriate content.

My grandmother did not _____ my mother to _____ until she

was _____ .

Be an Academic Author   **Work independently** to write two sentences. In your first sentence, use **permit** with the adverb of frequency *sometimes*. In your second sentence, use **permit** in the *simple present tense*.

❶ _____

_____

❷ _____

_____

> ### grammar tip
>
> Adverbs of frequency are words that show how often something happens. They usually go before the main verb.
>
> Teachers <u>sometimes</u> **permit** students to use dictionaries.
>
> He <u>often gets</u> tired after lunch.

Write an Academic Paragraph   **Complete** the paragraph using the correct form of **permit** and original content.

Children who are stars when they are _____
                                                        ❶

often grow up to be troubled adults. Parents of famous children often

_____ them to do things most _____
              ❷   ❸

aren't permitted to do. Just because they are famous, bars and clubs may

_____ child stars to enter even though they are too young. Child
          ❹

stars may spend a lot of time around people who are a lot older than they are, which isn't

always a good thing. Too much money can also _____ young
                                                              ❺

kids to follow their dreams—even the ones that aren't so good. If they want an expensive

_____ , for example, they can just buy one. It may look like fun to be a
          ❻

_____ , but too often their light burns out too soon.
          ❼

phase
noun

▶ **Say it:** phase

Write it: _____

Academic Vocabulary Toolkit

Meaning	Example
a stage or step in a process; a period of time in which someone or something changes or develops **Synonyms:** stage, step	The adult alligator is _____ , but in its first **phases** of development, it is rather _____ .

Forms	Family
• *Singular:* phase • *Plural:* phases	• *Verb:* phase

Word Partners	
• enter a new _____	With the signing of the agreement, relations between the two countries **enter a new phase**.
• final _____	Construction of our new house is in its **final phase**; we will be able to move in soon.

Verbal Practice

Talk about It **Read** each sentence and **think** about how you would complete it.

Discuss your idea with your partner using the sentence frame.

Listen carefully to your partner's and classmates' ideas.

Write your favorite idea in the blank.

❶ The final **phase** of a writing assignment includes _____ .

❷ Middle school and high school are important **phases** in your

_____ .

Writing Practice

Collaborate **Work with your partner** to complete the sentence using the correct form of **phase** and appropriate content.

Most people enter a new _____ of life when they _____ .

Your Turn **Work independently** to complete the sentence using the correct form of **phase** and appropriate content.

Building a _____ does not happen overnight; it involves several

_____ .

Be an Academic Author **Work independently** to write two sentences. In your first sentence, use **phase** in the *singular form* and include a word partner. In your second sentence, use **phase** in the *plural form* and include the quantifier *several*.

❶ _____

_____

❷ _____

_____

> **grammar tip**
>
> Quantifiers are words that tell us how much or how many of something there is. They usually come before the noun they describe.
>
> A frog's life has **several phases**.
>
> There are **numerous mistakes** in your paper.

Write an Academic Paragraph **Complete** the paragraph using the correct form of **phase** and original content.

Buying something in a store may seem simple, but it is really only one

_____ in a long process. The first phase of the buying
❶

process is recognizing that you need or _____ something.
❷

The second _____ is finding out how or where you can
❸

meet this need. If you want new shoes, will you buy them online, at a large discount

store, or at a _____ at the mall? Will you buy them now or
❹

_____ ? Even after you buy your shoes, the process isn't over.
❺

Another phase of the buying _____ occurs after you make your
❻

purchase. Are you happy with what you bought? Stores and companies are interested

in all _____ of the buying process. They want happy, satisfied
❼

_____ .
❽

potential
adjective

Academic Vocabulary Toolkit

Meaning	Example
able to become a kind of person or thing **Synonyms:** possible, likely	High _____ are a **potential** _____ to athletes.

Family

- *Noun:* potential
- *Adverb:* potentially

Word Partners

- _____ benefit(s) — There seem to be many **potential benefits** to drinking green tea.
- _____ problem(s) — Not getting enough vitamin B12 is a **potential problem** for people who don't eat meat.
- _____ risk(s) — Scientists are studying the **potential** risks of cell phone use.

Verbal Practice

Talk about It   **Read** each sentence and **think** about how you would complete it.

Discuss your idea with your partner using the sentence frame.

Listen carefully to your partner's and classmates' ideas.

Write your favorite idea in the blank.

❶ A **potential** risk when riding a bike is that you might _____ .

❷ If all students were required to buy e-books instead of textbooks,

_____ could be a **potential** problem.

Writing Practice

Collaborate   **Work with your partner** to complete the sentence using **potential** and appropriate content.

Our class is full of _____ doctors and _____ who just need

_____ to achieve their goals.

Your Turn   **Work independently** to complete the sentence using **potential** and appropriate content.

Before scientists can release a new _____ , they must first weigh the

_____ risks against the _____ benefits.

Be an   **Work independently** to write two sentences. In your first sentence, use **potential** with a *singular noun*.
Academic   In your second sentence, use **potential** with a *plural noun*. Use a word partner in one sentence.
Author

❶ _____

_____

❷ _____

_____

> **grammar tip**
>
> An adjective usually comes before the noun it describes.
>
> a **potential** benefit
>
> a **special** friendship
>
> **terrible** nightmares

Write an   **Complete** the paragraph using **potential** and original content.
Academic
Paragraph   We all love our cell phones, but some scientists believe that our phones pose a

_____ danger. Using _____ exposes us to
　　　　　　❶　　　　　　　　　　　　　　　　❷

radiation. These scientists say that this radiation could damage brain cells. Until we know for

sure, there are a few things you can do to limit any _____ injury.
　　　　　　　　　　　　　　　　　　　　　　　❸

When possible, use a _____ or a speakerphone. This will prevent you
　　　　　　　　　　　❹

from holding your phone right up to your _____ and will cut down
　　　　　　　　　　　　　　　　　　　　❺

your radiation exposure. Children should be especially careful. Their skulls are thinner and their

brains are still _____ . This could put them at a potentially greater risk
　　　　　　　　❻

of harm. To avoid _____ injury to their young brains, children should
　　　　　　　　❼

use cell phones as little as possible.

preparation
noun

Say it: prep • a • **ra** • tion   **Write it:** _____

Meaning	Example
the act of getting something ready to use **Synonyms:** planning, arrangement	Moving to a new _____ takes a lot of **preparation**.

Family

- **Verb:** prepare
- **Adjective:** prepared, preparatory

Word Partners

- adequate _____ You will do fine in algebra because you have had **adequate preparation**.
- careful _____ Sheila's **careful preparation** helped the party go smoothly.

Verbal Practice

Talk about It **Read** each sentence and **think** about how you would complete it.

Discuss your idea with your partner using the sentence frame.

Listen carefully to your partner's and classmates' ideas.

Write your favorite idea in the blank.

❶ Education is part of your **preparation** for _____ .

❷ Some people believe that **preparation** for college should begin in

_____.

Writing Practice

Collaborate | **Work with your partner** to complete the sentence using the correct form of **preparation** and appropriate content.

Careful _____ will come in handy if a disaster like a _____ or

a _____ ever hits your town.

Your Turn | **Work independently** to complete the sentence using the correct form of **preparation** and appropriate content.

The coach said that adequate _____ was the key to _____ .

Be an Academic Author | **Work independently** to write two sentences. In your first sentence, use **preparation** with the word partner *adequate preparation*. In your second sentence, use **preparation** with the word partner *careful preparation*.

❶ _____

_____

❷ _____

_____

> ## grammar tip
>
> **Non-count nouns name things that can't be counted. Non-count nouns have only one form. Do not add an −s to a non-count noun.**
>
> **Preparation** for a test includes a good breakfast.
>
> The **water** in the lake is frozen.

Write an Academic Paragraph | **Complete** the paragraph using the correct form of **preparation** and original content.

"Be prepared" is the motto of the Boy Scouts of America—and it's good advice for anyone who

is going camping. Careful _____ will make your camping experience
                                          ❶

much more _____ . First, make a detailed list of everything you think you
                  ❷

will need. Make sure you have a _____ that doesn't leak. You will also
                                        ❸

need a good sleeping bag and a mat to go under it to _____ you from
                                                              ❹

rocks and bumps in the ground. You will need at least one _____ with
                                                                  ❺

batteries. Don't forget to bring _____ in case of mosquitoes. Adequate
                                        ❻

_____ will save you from many uncomfortable moments.
        ❼

present
verb

Say it: pre • **sent**   **Write it:** _____

Academic Vocabulary Toolkit

Meaning	Example
to give someone something	The coach **presented** Julian with an _____ for his achievement in _____ .
Synonyms: introduce, show	

Forms	Family
Present: I/You/We/They present He/She/It presents **Past:** presented	• **Noun:** presentation • **Adjective:** presented

Word Partners

- _____ a challenge   Budget cuts **present a challenge** to public schools.
- _____ an opportunity   The museum's "Free Fridays" **present an opportunity** for everyone to see its collection.

Verbal Practice

Talk about It   **Read** each sentence and **think** about how you would complete it.

Discuss your idea with your partner using the sentence frame.

Listen carefully to your partner's and classmates' ideas.

Write your favorite idea in the blank.

❶ Today, learning _____ is **presenting** a challenge to our class.

❷ Students at our school are going to **present** a program about

_____ .

Writing Practice

Collaborate   **Work with your partner** to complete the sentence using the correct form of **present** and appropriate content.

The class trip _____ the opportunity to learn more about _____ .

Your Turn   **Work independently** to complete the sentence using the correct form of **present** and appropriate content.

When I write, I _____ my ideas in a clear and _____ manner.

Be an Academic Author   **Work independently** to write two sentences. In your first sentence, use **present** in the *present progressive tense*. In your second sentence, use **present** in the *past tense* and include a word partner.

❶ _____

_____

❷ _____

_____

> **grammar tip**
>
> **The present progressive tense is formed with *am/is/are* + verb ending in *–ing*.**
>
> I **am presenting** my new plan today.
>
> She **is running** down the street.

Write an Academic Paragraph   **Complete** the paragraph using the correct form of **present** and original content.

Extreme heat and humidity can _____ people with a number
❶

of problems. They can also make it difficult for machinery to work properly. In the late

1800s, printing plants suffered because heat and _____ caused
❷

problems with the paper and ink. Then, in 1902, Willis Carrier, a young employee at a printing

_____ in Brooklyn, New York, _____ his boss
❸   ❹

with a new invention that would _____ this problem: the electric air
❺

conditioner. His achievement came just one year after he had _____
❻

from Cornell University. Carrier's invention was so important that he was later

_____ with a medal for achievement in science.
❼

primary
adjective

Say it: **pri** • mar • y   **Write it:** _____

Academic Vocabulary Toolkit

Meaning	Example
most important **Synonyms:** principal, main	The **primary** _____ of cell phones used to be to make calls, but now _____ mostly use them to do other things!

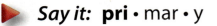

Family

• **Adverb:** primarily

Word Partners

• _____ reason   Jordan's **primary reason** for going to Spain is to learn Spanish.

• _____ goal   The **primary goal** of the bake sale is to raise money for the library.

Verbal Practice

Talk about It   **Read** each sentence and **think** about how you would complete it.

Discuss your idea with your partner using the sentence frame.

Listen carefully to your partner's and classmates' ideas.

Write your favorite idea in the blank.

❶ For me, the **primary** functions of a computer are to _____

and _____ .

❷ My **primary** goal in studying English is to be able to _____ .

Writing Practice

Collaborate   **Work with your partner** to complete the sentence using **primary** and appropriate content.

The _____ responsibility of a government is to _____ .

Your Turn   **Work independently** to complete the sentence using **primary** and appropriate content.

The _____ reason some students don't like school is that

_____ .

Be an Academic Author   **Work independently** to write two sentences. In your first sentence, use **primary** with a *singular noun* and include a word partner. In your second sentence, use **primary** with a *plural noun*.

❶ _____

_____

❷ _____

_____

> ### grammar tip
> An adjective usually comes before the noun it describes.
> a **primary** reason
> a **big** house
> a **green** jacket

Write an Academic Paragraph   **Complete** the paragraph using **primary** and original content.

The _____❶ purpose for getting an annual physical is to make sure

that your general health is good. Your _____❷ will usually listen to your

heartbeat, take your _____❸ pressure, check your reflexes, and weigh

you to make sure your weight is not below or above a _____❹ range. He

or she will also check your eyes and look into your ears. Your doctor may take blood and urine

samples to check your blood sugar and _____❺ levels. If your doctor finds

any _____❻ , he or she may prescribe medication. You may not enjoy your

visits to the doctor, but they are of _____❼ importance in the prevention

of serious illnesses.

principle
noun

Say it: **prin** · ci · ple   *Write it:* _____

Meaning	Example
a basic rule or idea about what is right *Synonyms:* standard, policy, belief	One of our _____ basic **principles** is _____ for every student.

RESPECT · INTEGRITY · EDUCATION

MILLER HIGH SCHOOL

Forms	Family
• *Singular:* principle • *Plural:* principles	• *Adjective:* principled

Word Partners	
• basic _____	Two of the **basic principles** of being a good parent are establishing rules and setting limits.
• matter of _____	As a **matter of principle**, I would never join a club if my friends weren't allowed to join as well.

Verbal Practice

Talk about It   **Read** each sentence and **think** about how you would complete it.

Discuss your idea with your partner using the sentence frame.

Listen carefully to your partner's and classmates' ideas.

Write your favorite idea in the blank.

❶ I refuse to wear _____ as a matter of **principle**.

❷ One of the basic **principles** of being a good friend is _____ .

Writing Practice

Collaborate **Work with your partner** to complete the sentence using the correct form of **principle** and appropriate content.

It isn't always easy to stick to your _____ , because there can be situations

where you might _____ .

Your Turn **Work independently** to complete the sentence using the correct form of **principle** and appropriate content.

One _____ that every coach should remember is that

_____ .

Be an Academic Author **Work independently** to write two sentences. In your first sentence, use **principle** in the *singular form*. In your second sentence, use **principle** in the *plural form*. Use a word partner in one sentence.

❶ _____

_____

❷ _____

_____

> **grammar tip**
>
> **Count nouns name things that can be counted. Count nouns have two forms, singular and plural. To make most count nouns plural, add –s.**
>
> Two basic principle**s** of music are rhythm and melody.
>
> He likes to play board game**s**.

Write an Academic Paragraph **Complete** the paragraph using the correct form of **principle** and original content.

It is important for teachers to have strong

_____ because they are role models
❶

for students. Teachers need to demonstrate qualities such as honesty and

_____ . For example, what should a teacher do when he or she sees
❷

a student cheating? Perhaps the student was sick or has _____
❸

at home. The teacher may feel _____ for the student and want
❹

to ignore the cheating. However, as a _____ of principle, the
❺

teacher needs to show that honesty is more important than _____ .
❻

Ignoring _____ will not help students in the end. Sticking to your
❼

_____ isn't always easy; but ultimately, it is the right thing to do.
❽

147

prior
adjective

Academic Vocabulary Toolkit

Meaning	Example	
earlier **Synonym:** previous	Angie's first job as a _____ required no **prior** _____ .	Dishwasher Wanted No prior experience necessary

Family

- *Noun:* priority
- *Verb:* prioritize

Word Partners

• _____ experience	We hired Lucy as a babysitter because of her **prior experience**; she has been babysitting for ten years.
• _____ knowledge	Use your **prior knowledge** of how people act to guess what the character will do next.
• _____ years	Unlike **prior years**, this year our baseball team had a winning season.

Verbal Practice

Talk about It **Read** each sentence and **think** about how you would complete it.

Discuss your idea with your partner using the sentence frame.

Listen carefully to your partner's and classmates' ideas.

Write your favorite idea in the blank.

① In **prior** years, _____ was the most popular kind of music.

Now _____ is more popular.

② I was surprised when _____ ; I had no **prior**

knowledge of their plans.

Writing Practice

Collaborate   **Work with your partner** to complete the sentence using **prior** and appropriate content.

I don't think I can get a job as a _____ because I don't have any

_____ experience.

Your Turn   **Work independently** to complete the sentence using **prior** and appropriate content.

When you begin studying _____ , your _____ knowledge of

_____ will help you because the two subjects are related.

Be an Academic Author   **Work independently** to write two sentences. In your first sentence, use **prior** with a *singular noun* and include a word partner. In your second sentence, use **prior** with a *plural noun*.

❶ _____

_____

❷ _____

_____

> **grammar tip**
>
> Adjectives do not have plural forms. Do not add –*s* to adjectives when they describe plural nouns.
>
> prior years
>
> loud dogs

Write an Academic Paragraph   **Complete** the paragraph using **prior** and original content.

Taking tests can be stressful. Your _____ experience ❶

taking tests has probably taught you a lot. Now, use what you know about yourself to

_____ ahead. If you get nervous before tests, begin by taking a deep ❷

_____ . Tell yourself that you will _____ . If ❸ ❹

you are easily distracted, try to choose a seat where you can focus. If there is a student who likes

to _____ sitting near you, move. In addition, read the test directions ❺

carefully before answering any _____ . You might want to answer the ❻

_____ questions first. If you have trouble answering a question, use your ❼

_____ knowledge of the subject. You never know when information ❽

from earlier classes can be useful!

process

noun

▶ **Say it: proc · ess**   *Write it:* _____

Academic Vocabulary Toolkit

Meaning	Example
a series of actions or changes *Synonyms:* system, plan, procedure	The **process** of getting a driver's _____ usually includes taking a _____ test.

Forms	Family
• *Singular:* process • *Plural:* processes	• *Verb:* process

Word Partners	
• complex _____	Getting a driver's license can be a **complex process** with many different steps.
• describe the _____	The test asked us to **describe the process** by which fossils are formed.
• slow _____	Some people learn to ice skate easily; for me, it was a long, **slow process**.

Verbal Practice

Talk about It **Read** each sentence and **think** about how you would complete it.

Discuss your idea with your partner using the sentence frame.

Listen carefully to your partner's and classmates' ideas.

Write your favorite idea in the blank.

❶ Part of the college application **process** is to _____ .

❷ It can be helpful to use words such as *first* and _____ when you are describing a complex **process**.

Writing Practice

Collaborate **Work with your partner** to complete the sentence using the correct form of **process** and appropriate content.

In science, we learn about many _____ , such as _____ and

_____ .

Your Turn **Work independently** to complete the sentence using the correct form of **process** and appropriate content.

Learning _____ can be a slow _____ .

Be an Academic Author **Work independently** to write two sentences. In your first sentence, use **process** in the *singular form* and include a word partner. In your second sentence, use **process** in the *plural form* with the quantifier *many*.

❶ _____

_____

❷ _____

_____

> **grammar tip**
>
> Quantifiers describe how much or how many of a noun there is.
>
> **Many** **processes** in science are quite complex.
>
> This store sells **various** **brands** of clothes.

Write an Academic Paragraph **Complete** the paragraph using the correct form of **process** and original content.

Have you ever watched little children working on an art project? Using

_____ ❶ , they watch how the colors combine. The final

_____ ❷ is not usually great art, but the activity is still important.

This is true for many situations in life; the _____ ❸ is more

important than the product. When students work on a group project or play on the

_____ ❹ team, the process of working together can be more valuable

than getting an A or _____ ❺ . Even the painful process of breaking up

with a _____ ❻ can be useful; it can show you what to do differently the

next time. Most people look at a finished product to judge _____ ❼ . But

when you recognize that the _____ ❽ is important, you won't worry as

much about the end result!

promote
verb

▶ **Say it:** pro • **mote**   **Write it:** _____

Meanings	Examples	
1. give someone a better job	**1.** Ella's boss recently **promoted her** to _____ of the company.	**CONGRATULATIONS ON YOUR PROMOTION!**
2. help something to happen	**2.** New _____ can **promote** learning.	

Forms	Family
Present: I/You/We/They promote He/She/It promotes **Past:** promoted	• **Noun:** promotion

Word Partners	
• ____ development	That organization works to **promote development** in poorer countries.
• ____ growth	He believes that lower taxes will **promote growth** in the economy.

Verbal Practice

Talk about It   **Read** each sentence and **think** about how you would complete it.

Discuss your idea with your partner using the sentence frame.

Listen carefully to your partner's and classmates' ideas.

Write your favorite idea in the blank.

❶ Companies don't **promote** people who _____ .

❷ If I wasn't **promoted** after working someplace for _____ ,

I would probably _____ .

❸ _____ are foods that **promote** good health.

❹ Art and music **promote** the development of _____ .

Writing Practice

Collaborate **Work with your partner** to complete the sentence using the correct form of **promote** and appropriate content.

Our school has _____ healthy eating by _____ .

Your Turn **Work independently** to complete the sentence using the correct form of **promote** and appropriate content.

You can help _____ world peace by _____ .

Be an Academic Author **Work independently** to write two sentences using Meaning 2. In your first sentence, use **promote** in the *present perfect tense*. In your second sentence, use **promote** with the *simple present tense* and include a word partner.

❶ _____

_____

❷ _____

_____

> ### grammar tip
>
> **The present perfect tense is formed with *has/have* + the past participle form of the verb. To make the past participle of regular verbs, add *–d* or *–ed*.**
>
> That group has promote**d** development in Africa.
>
> She has play**ed** basketball for years.

Write an Academic Paragraph **Complete** the paragraph using the correct form of **promote** and original content.

One of the most famous children's television shows in the United

States is *Sesame Street*. *Sesame Street* is a show that _____ literacy.
                                                                                    ❶

The show is set on a _____ street where human actors and puppets
                                              ❷

interact. Celebrities such as _____ often come on the show, which
                                              ❸

makes older children and parents also want to watch. Since it started in 1969, *Sesame*

Street has helped millions of children learn to _____ and count.
                                                                      ❹

Sesame Street doesn't only _____ children letters and numbers,
                                              ❺

however. The producers also _____ respect for differences and kids'
                                              ❻

self-esteem. The show helps _____ awareness of disabilities; one
                                              ❼

character, for example, uses a wheelchair. Most children, of course, just want to watch

Sesame Street to see the funny _____ !
                                                    ❽

rational
adjective

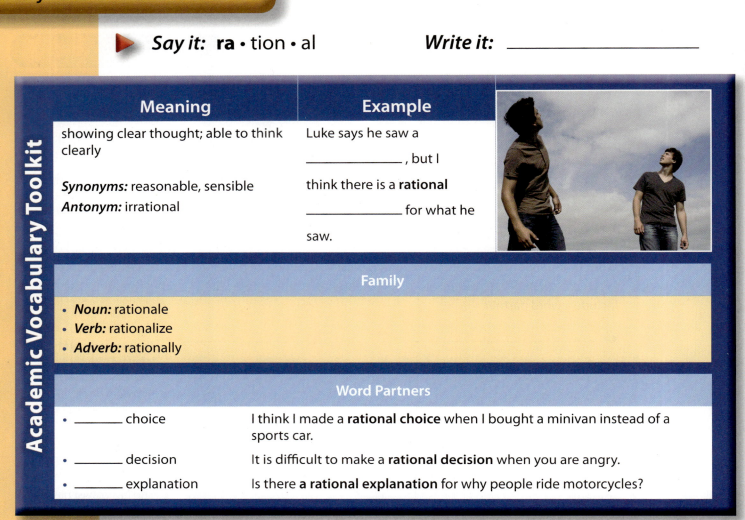

Academic Vocabulary Toolkit

Meaning	Example
showing clear thought; able to think clearly *Synonyms:* reasonable, sensible *Antonym:* irrational	Luke says he saw a _____ , but I think there is a **rational** _____ for what he saw.

Family

- *Noun:* rationale
- *Verb:* rationalize
- *Adverb:* rationally

Word Partners

- _____ choice — I think I made a **rational choice** when I bought a minivan instead of a sports car.
- _____ decision — It is difficult to make a **rational decision** when you are angry.
- _____ explanation — Is there **a rational explanation** for why people ride motorcycles?

Verbal Practice

Talk about It **Read** each sentence and **think** about how you would complete it.

Discuss your idea with your partner using the sentence frame.

Listen carefully to your partner's and classmates' ideas.

Write your favorite idea in the blank.

❶ If you tell someone that they aren't being **rational**, it usually makes them

_____ .

❷ **Rational** explanations of UFOs are that they are _____ or

_____ .

Writing Practice

Collaborate **Work with your partner** to complete the sentence using **rational** and appropriate content.

It can be difficult to make a _____ decision about

_____ .

Your Turn **Work independently** to complete the sentence using **rational** and appropriate content.

I believe that voting for _____ is the only _____ choice.

Be an Academic Author **Work independently** to write two sentences. In your first sentence, use **rational** with a *plural noun*. In your second sentence, use **rational** with the word partner *rational explanation*.

❶ _____

_____

❷ _____

_____

> **grammar tip**
>
> **Adjectives do not have plural forms. Do not add –s to adjectives when they describe plural nouns.**
>
> <u>rational</u> explanations
> <u>loud</u> dogs

Write an Academic Paragraph **Complete** the paragraph using **rational** and original content.

Most of us are afraid of something. Some fears are _____ ❶ ; it is logical

to be careful in dangerous situations. There are rational _____ ❷ for being

scared of fire or violence. However, some fears are not _____ ❸ . Irrational,

extreme fears are called *phobias*. People can have phobias of just about anything, even things that

seem safe, such as bunnies or _____ ❹ . Someone with a phobia of clowns,

for example, will probably refuse to go to the _____ ❺ . Other people have

_____ ❻ that seriously affect their daily life. They might be afraid to leave

the house or refuse to touch anything out of a fear of _____ ❼ . These fears

can have a serious effect on the person with the phobia and on the _____ ❽

who love them.

regular
adjective

▶ *Say it:* **reg** • u • lar   *Write it:* _____

<table>
<tr><th colspan="2">Meanings</th><th>Examples</th></tr>
<tr><td colspan="2">1. ordinary, not unusual</td><td>1. My _____ drives a sports car, but my _____ drives a **regular** car.</td></tr>
<tr><td colspan="2">2. always happening at the same time or after the same amount of time has passed

Antonym: irregular</td><td>2. It's _____ to get **regular** _____ cleanings and examinations.</td></tr>
</table>

Family
- *Noun:* regularity
- *Adverb:* regularly

Word Partners
• _____ basis	I almost never get to go to concerts, but Mark and Nina go on a **regular basis**.
• _____ schedule	My **regular** work **schedule** is Friday and Saturday, 5:00 to 10:00.

Academic Vocabulary Toolkit

Verbal Practice

Talk about It **Read** each sentence and **think** about how you would complete it.

Discuss your idea with your partner using the sentence frame.

Listen carefully to your partner's and classmates' ideas.

Write your favorite idea in the blank.

❶ I wear special clothes to _____ , but I just wear **regular** clothes to _____ .

❷ _____ is a **regular** guy who never shows off.

❸ Our school cafeteria serves _____ on a **regular** basis.

❹ **Regular** visits to the _____ should be part of your life.

Writing Practice

Collaborate **Work with your partner** to complete the sentence using **regular** and appropriate content.

Because of the first-period ＿＿＿＿＿＿＿＿＿＿＿＿＿＿ , we will not follow the

＿＿＿＿＿＿＿＿＿＿＿＿＿＿ class schedule today.

Your Turn **Work independently** to complete the sentence using **regular** and appropriate content.

I go online and update my ＿＿＿＿＿＿＿＿＿＿＿ on a ＿＿＿＿＿＿＿＿＿＿＿

basis.

Be an Academic Author **Work independently** to write two sentences using Meaning 2. In your first sentence, use **regular** with a *plural noun*. In your second sentence, use **regular** with a *singular noun*. Include a word partner in one sentence.

❶ ＿＿＿＿＿＿＿＿＿＿＿＿＿＿＿＿＿＿＿＿＿＿＿＿

＿＿＿＿＿＿＿＿＿＿＿＿＿＿＿＿＿＿＿＿＿＿＿＿

❷ ＿＿＿＿＿＿＿＿＿＿＿＿＿＿＿＿＿＿＿＿＿＿＿＿

＿＿＿＿＿＿＿＿＿＿＿＿＿＿＿＿＿＿＿＿＿＿＿＿

> ### grammar tip
>
> Adjectives do not have plural forms. Do not add an –*s* to adjectives when they describe plural nouns.
> regular visits
> puffy marshmallows

Write an Academic Paragraph **Complete** the paragraph using **regular** and original content.

    If you're like most Americans, you probably take a shower or bath every day—maybe

even more than once a day! But is this much bathing really ＿＿＿＿＿＿＿＿＿＿＿
❶

—or good for us? Of course, ＿＿＿＿＿＿＿＿＿＿＿ bathing is necessary for
❷

good health and hygiene. However, daily bathing can actually damage the skin and wash

away ＿＿＿＿＿＿＿＿＿＿＿ oils. Similarly, daily shampooing can damage your
❸

＿＿＿＿＿＿＿＿＿＿＿ . In addition, over-bathing can also ＿＿＿＿＿＿＿＿＿＿＿
❹   ❺

the environment. A ten-minute shower uses 20 to 25 gallons of water. If you shower for ten

minutes every day, you use 140 to 175 gallons per ＿＿＿＿＿＿＿＿＿＿＿ ! You might
❻

want to consider making **not** washing your hair part of your ＿＿＿＿＿＿＿＿＿＿＿
❼

schedule.

regulation
noun

Say it: reg • u • **la** • tion   **Write it:** _____

Academic Vocabulary Toolkit

Meanings	Examples
1. an official rule *Synonym:* rule	**1.** The student _____ lists all of the _____ and **regulations** of the school.
2. the act of controlling something	**2.** The United States Department of Agriculture is _____ for the **regulation** of the agricultural _____ .

Forms	Family
• *Singular:* regulation • *Plural:* regulations	• *Verb:* regulate • *Adjective:* regulated, regulatory

Word Partners	
• government _____	There are many **government regulations** concerning food safety.
• subject to _____	The airline industry is **subject to regulation** by the government.

Verbal Practice

Talk about It   **Read** each sentence and **think** about how you would complete it.

Discuss your idea with your partner using the sentence frame.

Listen carefully to your partner's and classmates' ideas.

Write your favorite idea in the blank.

❶ Our school's **regulations** do not allow students to

_____ .

❷ I do not think we should have a **regulation** against

_____ .

❸ The **regulation** of _____ is important for public health.

❹ I think _____ should be subject to strict government

regulation.

Writing Practice

Collaborate **Work with your partner** to complete the sentences using the correct form of **regulation** and appropriate content.

1. Safety _____ are important in places such as _____ .

2. A government agency is responsible for the _____ of _____ .

Your Turn **Work independently** to complete the sentences using the correct form of **regulation** and appropriate content.

1. If I were the mayor of _____ , I would issue a _____ to

_____ .

2. Many buildings were destroyed in the _____ due to the lack of

_____ of the _____ industry.

Be an **Work independently** to write two sentences. In your first sentence, use **regulation** in the *plural form*. In
Academic your second sentence, use **regulation** in the *singular form* and include a word partner.
Author

MEANING
1. _____

_____

MEANING
2. _____

_____

> ### grammar tip
>
> Count nouns name things that can be counted. To make most count nouns plural, add –s. The first meaning of *regulation* is a count noun. The second meaning of *regulation* is a non-count noun.

Write an **Complete** the paragraph using the correct form of **regulation** and original
Academic content.
Paragraph

Before the beginning of the twentieth century, there were few _____

❶

in the United States concerning child labor. Employers could hire _____

❷

of any age. There was also no _____ of how many

❸

_____ per day children could work. Factories had workers as

❹

young as six or seven who worked more than 40 hours a week. Today, young people are

protected by government _____ concerning child labor. Generally,

❺

today's laws set 14 as the _____ age for employment. However,

❻

_____ allow children of any age to be employed by their parents to

❼

work on a family farm.

resolution
noun

Academic Vocabulary Toolkit

Meanings	Examples	
1. a promise to do or not do something	**1.** Bella's New Year's **resolution** was to _____ less time on the _____ .	
2. the solution to a problem or difficulty	**2.** When the _____ did not get along, the only **resolution** was for one of them to _____ out.	

Forms	Family
• *Singular:* resolution • *Plural:* resolutions	• *Verb:* resolve • *Adjective:* resolute, resolved • *Adverb:* resolutely

Word Partners	
• peaceful _____	Everyone was happy to hear of the **peaceful resolution** to the problem.

Verbal Practice

Talk about It **Read** each sentence and **think** about how you would complete it.

Discuss your idea with your partner using the sentence frame.

Listen carefully to your partner's and classmates' ideas.

Write your favorite idea in the blank.

❶ My New Year's **resolution** next year will be to _____ .

❷ I think all kids my age should make a **resolution** to _____ .

❸ It's difficult to find successful **resolutions** to complex problems like _____ .

❹ My best friend and I had an argument about _____ , but we came to a peaceful **resolution**.

Writing Practice

Collaborate   **Work with your partner** to complete the sentence using the correct form of **resolution** and appropriate content.

I think the best _____ to a story is one in which the main character

_____ .

Your Turn   **Work independently** to complete the sentence using the correct form of **resolution** and appropriate content.

Major nations need to work together to find a _____ to the problem

of _____ .

Be an Academic Author   **Work independently** to write two sentences using Meaning 2. In your first sentence, use **resolution** in the *singular form* and include a word partner. In your second sentence, use **resolution** in the *plural form*.

❶ _____

_____

❷ _____

_____

Write an Academic Paragraph   **Complete** the paragraph using the correct form of **resolution** and original content.

Different people approach conflict differently. Some people

avoid _____ ❶ , pretending that problems don't exist while hoping

they will disappear. Some people are completely uncompromising. They place their own

_____ ❷ above everything and everyone else. Other people are extremely

accommodating; the _____ ❸ to every problem lies in their giving up

everything while others give up _____ ❹ . Are any of these the best

way to come to a _____ ❺ of important problems? Of course not. In the

best _____ ❻ resolution, individuals work together toward a common

goal. When everyone communicates equally, sharing ideas and responsibilities, a lasting

_____ ❼ can be reached.

resolve
verb

▶ **Say it:** re · **solve**   **Write it:** _____

Meanings	Examples
1. to decide to do something *Synonyms:* determine, promise	**1.** Mimi **resolved** to start _____ on New Year's Day.
2. to find a solution to a problem or argument *Synonyms:* solve, fix, settle	**2.** Mrs. Watkins quickly **resolved** the _____ about who would sit in the front seat.

Forms		Family
Present: I/You/We/They resolve He/She/It resolves *Past:* resolved		• *Adjective:* resolute, resolved • *Adverb:* resolutely

Word Partners
• _____ a problem   Before you can **resolve a problem**, you must understand what the problem is.
• _____ the/an issue   The Thirteenth Amendment **resolved the issue** of slavery once and for all.

Verbal Practice

Talk about It **Read** each sentence and **think** about how you would complete it.

Discuss your idea with your partner using the sentence frame.

Listen carefully to your partner's and classmates' ideas.

Write your favorite idea in the blank.

❶ This week, I have **resolved** to _____ .

❷ People who lead unhealthy lives should **resolve** to _____ .

❸ I **resolve** differences with my friends by _____ .

❹ The countries **resolved** their problems by _____ .

162

Writing Practice

Collaborate   **Work with your partner** to complete the sentence using the correct form of **resolve** and appropriate content.

Some people _____ issues by _____ , while

others prefer to _____ .

Your Turn   **Work independently** to complete the sentence frame using the correct form of **resolve** and appropriate content.

The first issue the new president must _____ is the urgent problem of

_____ .

Be an Academic Author   **Work independently** to write two sentences using Meaning 2. In your first sentence, use **resolve** with the modal verb *must*. In your second sentence, use **resolve** in the simple past tense and include a word partner.

❶ _____

_____

❷ _____

_____

> ### grammar tip
>
> **Modal verbs give additional meaning to the main verb. *Must* expresses necessity.**
>
> We **must** **resolve** this problem.
>
> You **must** **hurry** or you will be late.

Write an Academic Paragraph   **Complete** the paragraph using the correct form of **resolve** and original content.

     In the American South in the 1700s, slaves labored on plantations that

_____ tobacco and cotton. However, toward the end of the eighteenth
       ❶

century, neither crop was very profitable, and slavery was _____ . Cotton
                                         ❷

was difficult to process because its sticky seeds needed to be _____
                                                                          ❸

by hand. Then, in 1794, Eli Whitney invented the cotton gin, a machine that removed cotton

seeds _____ . The cotton gin not only _____
      ❹   ❺

the basic problem of removing the seeds; it also turned cotton into a profitable crop. However,

not everyone enjoyed this success. By 1810, the number of slaves in the United States

_____ from around 700,000 to 1.2 million. Eli Whitney's invention
      ❻

_____ one problem only to create a much more serious problem.
      ❼

responsibility
noun

Say it: re • spon • si • **bil** • i • ty   **Write it:** _____

Meanings	Examples
1. something that you have to do, because it is your job or because it is the right thing to do **Synonyms:** duty, obligation **Antonym:** irresponsibility	1. All drivers have a **responsibility** to drive _____ and _____ the rules of the road.
2. blame for something bad	2. Alan and Skye _____ **responsibility** for not obeying the _____ .

Forms	Family
• **Singular:** responsibility • **Plural:** responsibilities	• **Adjective:** responsible • **Adverb:** responsibly

Word Partners	
• accept _____	When his six-year-old brother accidentally broke a window while playing ball with him, Steve **accepted responsibility**.
• sense of _____	A babysitting job can help a young teen develop a **sense of responsibility**.

Verbal Practice

Talk about It   **Read** each sentence and **think** about how you would complete it.

Discuss your idea with your partner using the sentence frame.

Listen carefully to your partner's and classmates' ideas.

Write your favorite idea in the blank.

❶ Parents have a **responsibility** to _____ their children.

❷ At home, _____ is my **responsibility**.

❸ It can be hard to accept **responsibility** for your _____ .

❹ Terrorists claimed **responsibility** for _____ .

Writing Practice

Collaborate **Work with your partner** to complete the sentences using the correct form of **responsibility** and appropriate content.

❶ Pet owners have a _____ to _____ .

❷ A company that causes a disaster, such as _____ , should take

_____ for the damage.

Your Turn **Work independently** to complete the sentences using the correct form of **responsibility** and appropriate content.

❶ Teachers have many _____ , including

_____ and _____ .

❷ _____ will help young people develop a sense of _____ .

Be an Academic Author **Work independently** to write two sentences. In your first sentence, use **responsibility** in the *plural form*. In your second sentence, use **responsibility** in the *singular form*. Include a word partner in one sentence.

MEANING ❶ _____

_____

MEANING ❷ _____

_____

> ### grammar tip
>
> Count nouns name things that can be counted. Count nouns have two forms, singular and plural. Meaning 1 of *responsibility* is a count noun.

Write an Academic Paragraph **Complete** the paragraph using the correct form of **responsibility** and original content.

"*She* started it!" "It's all *his* fault." "That's not *my* problem." When a difficult situation arises, many

people try to avoid accepting _____ . We don't want to feel bad about
　　　　　　　　　　　　　　　　　　❶

ourselves or _____ we have failed in some way. We also don't want
　　　　　　　❷

to have to do anything more than what is absolutely _____ . This way
　　　　　　　　　　　　　　　　　　　　　　　❸

of thinking starts early. Children need to develop a sense of _____
　　　　　　　　　　　　　　　　　　　　　　　　　　　❹

when they are young. It is a parent's _____ to teach children how their
　　　　　　　　　　　　　　❺

_____ can affect others. If we learn to _____
　　　❻　　　　　　　　　　　　　　　　　　　　❼

the part we play in each situation, then we will stop looking for someone else to take

_____ .
　　❽

role
noun

▶ **Say it:** role   **Write it:** _____

Academic Vocabulary Toolkit

Meanings	Examples
1. a part played by an actor or actress *Synonym:* character	1. Which _____ was chosen to play the **role** of the _____ ?
2. a part or job someone or something has in a group *Synonym:* position	2. _____ play an important **role** in a _____ ecosystem.

Forms

- *Singular:* role
- *Plural:* roles

Word Partners

• play a _____	My grandmother **played an important role** in my childhood; she was always there for me when I needed her.
• active _____	Jane takes an **active role** in school politics; she is on three different committees, and now she is running for class president.

Verbal Practice

Talk about It **Read** each sentence and **think** about how you would complete it.

Discuss your idea with your partner using the sentence frame.

Listen carefully to your partner's and classmates' ideas.

Write your favorite idea in the blank.

❶ In the school play, _____ played the **role** of _____ .

❷ _____ has a starring **role** in a new movie.

❸ Classes such as _____ play an important **role** in our education.

❹ As children grow, _____ take a variety of **roles** in their lives.

Writing Practice

Collaborate **Work with your partner** to complete the sentence using the correct form of **role** and appropriate content.

The _____ of student government should be to

_____ .

Your Turn **Work independently** to complete the sentence using the correct form of **role** and appropriate content.

_____ play an important _____ in shaping the behavior of

teenagers.

Be an Academic Author **Work independently** to write two sentences using Meaning 2. In your first sentence, use **role** in the *singular form* and include a word partner. In your second sentence, use **role** in the *plural form* with the quantifier *a variety of*.

❶ _____

_____

❷ _____

_____

> ### grammar tip
> Quantifiers are words that tell us how much or how many of something there is. They usually come before the noun they describe.
>
> Mr. Collins plays **a variety of** roles at our school.
>
> This restaurant has **numerous** options.

Write an Academic Paragraph **Complete** the paragraph using the correct form of **role** and original content.

The role of women has changed a lot over the last hundred years.

At the beginning of the _____ century, women in the United States
❶

could not vote. Today, women are running for _____ ! Not so
❷

long ago, it was a man's _____ to work and provide food and
❸

_____ for his family. A woman's role, on the other hand, was to stay
❹

home and take care of the _____ . While many women were active in
❺

their communities, it was usually through charity, such as _____ people
❻

in need. When women did have jobs outside the home, they were often asked to leave when they

got married. Today, women play an important _____ in the workforce,
❼

and most people can't imagine a time when women couldn't _____ .
❽

sequence
noun

▶ **Say it:** **se** • quence   **Write it:** _____

Meaning	Example
an order of events or things **Synonym:** series	In a _____ , the colors always appear in the same **sequence**, with red on top and _____ at the bottom.

Forms	Family
• **Singular:** sequence • **Plural:** sequences	• **Verb:** sequence • **Adjective:** sequential • **Adverb:** sequentially

Word Partners
• _____ of events   The police asked the witnesses about the **sequence of events** that led to the fight.

Verbal Practice

Talk about It   **Read** each sentence and **think** about how you would complete it.

Discuss your idea with your partner using the sentence frame.

Listen carefully to your partner's and classmates' ideas.

Write your favorite idea in the blank.

❶ I got confused when I read the _____ books out of **sequence**.

❷ Tests often ask students to put _____ in the correct **sequence**.

Writing Practice

Collaborate **Work with your partner** to complete the sentence using the correct form of **sequence** and appropriate content.

In math class, we had to find the next _____ in several different

_____ of numbers.

Your Turn **Work independently** to complete the sentence using the correct form of **sequence** and appropriate content.

The movies _____ and _____ both had a similar

_____ of events.

Be an Academic Author **Work independently** to write two sentences. In your first sentence, use **sequence** in the *singular form* with the word partner *sequence of events*. In your second sentence, use **sequence** in the *plural form* with the quantifier *several*.

❶ _____

_____

❷ _____

_____

> ### grammar tip
>
> Quantifiers are words that tell us how much or how many of something there is. They usually come before the noun they describe.
>
> I learned **several** **sequences** of steps for the dance competition.
>
> This restaurant has **a variety of** options.

Write an Academic Paragraph **Complete** the paragraph using the correct form of **sequence** and original content.

When you read about a _____ of events in history, it can be hard
            ❶

to remember all the dates. One way to learn these _____ is to make
                                    ❷

a timeline. A timeline puts all of the _____ on one page. To make a
                        ❸

_____ , first draw a horizontal line across the middle of a sheet of
        ❹

paper. Then write the date of the first _____ at the bottom of the
                        ❺

far left end of the line. Write the event above the date on the other side of the line. Do the

same for the other events, leaving an appropriate amount of _____
                                ❻

between events and dates. Now you have a visual representation of the correct

_____ of a series of historical _____ .
        ❼   ❽

series
noun

Say it: se • ries   **Write it:** _____

Meaning	Example
a group of similar things or events that follow each other in order **Synonym:** sequence	This _____ is expensive, but it is the _____ one in the **series**.

Family

- *Adjective:* serial
- *Adverb:* serially
- *Verb:* serialize

Word Partners

• _____ of events	In history, we learned about the **series of events** that led to the Civil War.
• _____ of steps	Science experiments require you to follow a **series of steps** in the correct order.

Verbal Practice

Talk about It   **Read** each sentence and **think** about how you would complete it.

Discuss your idea with your partner using the sentence frame.

Listen carefully to your partner's and classmates' ideas.

Write your favorite idea in the blank.

❶ I like watching several different **series** on TV, including _____ .

❷ In February, the library will have a **series** of events to celebrate _____ .

Writing Practice

Collaborate   **Work with your partner** to complete the sentence using **series** and appropriate content.

My favorite _____ of comic books is _____ .

Your Turn   **Work independently** to complete the sentence using **series** and appropriate content.

Each morning, I follow a _____ of steps to get ready for school; first I

_____ , then I _____ , and then I _____ .

Be an Academic Author   **Work independently** to write two sentences. In your first sentence, use **series** with a word partner. In your second sentence, use **series** with the quantifier *several*.

❶ _____

_____

❷ _____

_____

> ## grammar tip
>
> Quantifiers are words that tell us how much or how many of something there is. They usually come before the noun they describe.
>
> We took **several** series of tests.
>
> I have **a number of** coins in my pocket.

Write an Academic Paragraph   **Complete** the paragraph using **series** and original content.

Many of the books that are most popular with young adult readers are part of a

_____ . Who hasn't heard of that _____
    ❶   ❷

of books about the adventures of a certain wizard and his friends? Other popular series

are *The Lord of the Rings* books and the _____ series. Another
    ❸

set of serial novels is appropriately titled *A _____ of Unfortunate*
    ❹

Events. In a series, if you like the first book, you will probably like the rest. In the first

book, readers are introduced to the _____ and the setting. Once
    ❺

readers are hooked, they can read the rest of the books to learn more about the characters'

_____ and follow their development. A series allows writers to explore
    ❻

_____ in greater depth over a longer period of time and in many
    ❼

different situations.

solution
noun

Academic Vocabulary Toolkit

Meaning	Example
an answer to a problem **Synonym:** answer	Some teenagers have trouble _____ ; sticking to a _____ is one possible **solution**.

Forms	Family
• **Singular:** solution • **Plural:** solutions	• **Verb:** solve • **Adjective:** solvable

Word Partners

• find a/the _____	To **find the solution** to this math problem, you have to know how to multiply fractions.
• _____ to the problem	This update should be the **solution to the problem** you are having with the software.

Verbal Practice

Talk about It   **Read** each sentence and **think** about how you would complete it.

Discuss your idea with your partner using the sentence frame.

Listen carefully to your partner's and classmates' ideas.

Write your favorite idea in the blank.

❶ If a student always comes to class late, I think one possible **solution** is for the teacher

to _____ .

❷ If I don't know the **solution** to a math problem, I usually _____ .

Writing Practice

Collaborate **Work with your partner** to complete the sentence using the correct form of **solution** and appropriate content.

I suggested numerous _____ to his problems, but he just wanted to

_____ .

Your Turn **Work independently** to complete the sentence using the correct form of **solution** and appropriate content.

If I could find a _____ to one major problem in the world, I would want to

_____ .

Be an Academic Author **Work independently** to write two sentences. In your first sentence, use **solution** in the *singular form* and use a word partner. In your second sentence, use **solution** in the *plural form* with the quantifier *numerous*.

❶ _____

_____

❷ _____

_____

grammar tip

Quantifiers are words that tell us how much or how many of something there is. They usually come before the noun they describe.

There are **numerous** solutions to that problem.

A number of students wear jeans everyday.

Write an Academic Paragraph **Complete** the paragraph using the correct form of **solution** and original content.

Some problems have simple _____ .
❶

For example, if you are thirsty, you can have a drink. If you are tired, try to

_____ . Unfortunately, some problems seem to have
❷

no easy _____ . Problems such as troubles at home or
❸

_____ at school can be difficult to solve on your own. Trying to
❹

find an _____ solution can make you feel alone. One possible
❺

_____ is to talk about the problem with an adult you trust. When you
❻

talk to a responsible adult, such as _____ , you will have someone else
❼

to help you. You might be surprised; when they were younger, they might have had a problem

similar to yours.

solve
verb

▶ **Say it:** **solve**   **Write it:** _____

Meaning	Example
to find the correct answer to a question or problem	My teacher _____ me up to the board to **solve** the _____ problem.

Forms	Family
Present: I/You/We/They solve He/She/It solves **Past:** solved	• **Noun:** solution • **Adjective:** solvable

Word Partners

• _____ a/the mystery	Only a trained detective can **solve the mystery**.
• _____ a/the problem	A new pitcher may **solve the** team's **problem**.
• try to _____	I am **trying to solve** the puzzle without any help.

Verbal Practice

Talk about It **Read** each sentence and **think** about how you would complete it.

Discuss your idea with your partner using the sentence frame.

Listen carefully to your partner's and classmates' ideas.

Write your favorite idea in the blank.

❶ Our school could **solve** problems more effectively if it

_____ .

❷ Long ago, people **solved** math problems without _____ .

Writing Practice

Collaborate **Work with your partner** to complete the sentence using the correct form of **solve** and appropriate content.

The police _____ crimes using _____ and _____ .

Your Turn **Work independently** to complete the sentence using the correct form of **solve** and appropriate content.

I try to _____ problems by _____ .

Be an Academic Author **Work independently** to write two sentences. In your first sentence, use **solve** in the *simple present tense* with a person's name. In your second sentence, use **solve** in the *simple past tense* and include a word partner.

❶ _____

_____

❷ _____

_____

> ### grammar tip
> **In the simple present tense, the third person (*he/she/it*) form takes an −s or −es ending.**
>
> Sasha solve**s** complex math problems without a calculator.
>
> Mr. Tom teach**es** my biology class.

Write an Academic Paragraph **Complete** the paragraph using the correct form of **solve** and original content.

Autism is a disorder that _____ ❶ the development of the brain. About 10 percent of autistic people are *savants*. Savants have _____ ❷ mental abilities that allow them to do things normal people can't. For example, many savants can _____ ❸ complex math problems in their heads faster than most people can when using a calculator. Other savants can memorize books, play long passages of music after hearing them only once, or _____ ❹ several languages very quickly. No one is sure what causes autism or Savant syndrome; researchers are still trying to _____ ❺ those mysteries. Scientists do know that savants have some damage to the part of the brain that controls social and verbal _____ ❻ . Somehow these changes in the brain _____ ❼ savants with extraordinary abilities.

statement
noun

Say it: **state** • ment   *Write it:* _____

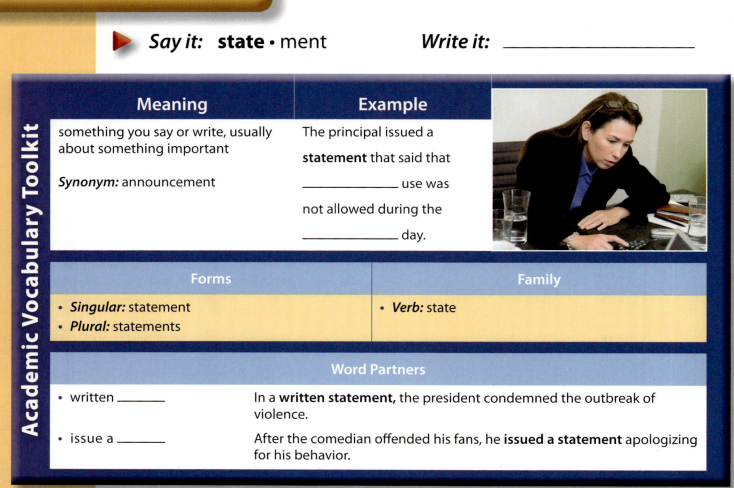

Academic Vocabulary Toolkit

Meaning	Example
something you say or write, usually about something important *Synonym:* announcement	The principal issued a **statement** that said that _____ use was not allowed during the _____ day.

Forms	Family
• *Singular:* statement • *Plural:* statements	• *Verb:* state

Word Partners

• written _____	In a **written statement,** the president condemned the outbreak of violence.
• issue a _____	After the comedian offended his fans, he **issued a statement** apologizing for his behavior.

Verbal Practice

Talk about It **Read** each sentence and **think** about how you would complete it.

Discuss your idea with your partner using the sentence frame.

Listen carefully to your partner's and classmates' ideas.

Write your favorite idea in the blank.

❶ After important games, coaches sometimes make **statements** explaining

_____ .

❷ When you write _____ , you should begin with a

clear **statement** of purpose.

Writing Practice

Collaborate **Work with your partner** to complete the sentence using the correct form of **statement** and appropriate content.

The celebrity issued a _____ to the press after _____ .

Your Turn **Work independently** to complete the sentence using the correct form of **statement** and appropriate content.

The television commercial made a number of misleading _____ about

_____ .

Be an Academic Author **Work independently** to write two sentences. In your first sentence, use **statement** in the *singular form*. In your second sentence, use **statement** in the *plural form* and include a word partner.

❶ _____

_____

❷ _____

_____

> ### grammar tip
>
> Count nouns name things that can be counted. Count nouns have two forms, singular and plural. To make most count nouns plural, add –*s*.
>
> His statement**s** are not truthful.
>
> She likes board games.

Write an Academic Paragraph **Complete** the paragraph using the correct form of **statement** and original content.

It is a staple of television news. An athlete, a politician, or a _____

❶

stands in front of a group of reporters and issues a _____ . In the

❷

_____ , the speaker offers an apology for some bad thing he or she got

❸

caught doing. You may never become famous, but at some time in your life, you too will have to

apologize to someone. When that time comes, make sure your _____ is

❹

sincere. In a sincere apology, you _____ that you did something wrong.

❺

You may try to explain why, but don't make _____ . Don't make the

❻

apology all about you. It's not important now how you feel. It's important how the other person

feels. You can never undo something that's done, but a sincere _____ of

❼

regret can help make things better.

strategy
noun

Say it: **stra** • te • gy   *Write it:* _____

Meaning	Example
a plan to reach a goal **Synonym:** plan	The _____ players listened carefully while their coach explained his new **strategy** for the _____ .

Forms	Family
• **Singular:** strategy • **Plural:** strategies	• **Verb:** strategize • **Adjective:** strategic • **Adverb:** strategically

Word Partners	
• develop a _____	As a community, we must **develop a strategy** for dealing with abandoned buildings.
• effective _____	If you want to advertise a yard sale, an **effective strategy** is to put up posters around your neighborhood.

Verbal Practice

Talk about It **Read** each sentence and **think** about how you would complete it.

Discuss your idea with your partner using the sentence frame.

Listen carefully to your partner's and classmates' ideas.

Write your favorite idea in the blank.

❶ If you don't want the teacher to call on you, an effective **strategy** is to

_____ .

❷ _____ is a game that involves a lot of **strategy**.

Writing Practice

Collaborate   **Work with your partner** to complete the sentence using the correct form of **strategy** and appropriate content.

The company developed new _____ to get people to

_____ .

Your Turn   **Work independently** to complete the sentence using the correct form of **strategy** and appropriate content.

An effective _____ for learning vocabulary is to _____ .

Be an Academic Author   **Work independently** to write two sentences. In your first sentence, use **strategy** in the *singular form*. In your second sentence, use **strategy** in the *plural form* and include a word partner.

❶ _____

_____

❷ _____

_____

> **grammar tip**
>
> To form the plural of a noun that ends in a consonant + *y*, change the *y* to *i* and add −*es*.
>
> strategy—strateg**ies**
>
> story—stor**ies**

Write an Academic Paragraph   **Complete** the paragraph using the correct form of **strategy** and original content.

    Many supermarkets have _____ to encourage customers to
                 ❶

spend more money. One _____ strategy is to put candy next
             ❷

to the cash register. Customers have to wait in line, and when they see candy, they

_____ it. Supermarkets also strategically place name-brand food at
     ❸

eye level. For example, in a cereal aisle, more expensive _____ will
                             ❹

be right where customers notice them most. Supermarkets also offer deals, such as "2 for $5."

Although you only need to buy _____ to get the discounted price,
              ❺

customers see "2" and then buy two items. However, supermarket customers can develop their

own _____ for saving money. The most _____
    ❻   ❼

supermarket money-saving strategy is to eat before you go food shopping. If you go to a

supermarket hungry, everything looks _____ !
                  ❽

substitute
verb

▶ **Say it:** **sub** • sti • tute   **Write it:** _____

Meaning	Example
to take the place of someone else, or to use something different instead of the usual thing **Synonym:** replace	Fans were surprised when the _____ **substituted** the star player for a _____ in the last five minutes of the big game.

Forms		Family
Present: I/You/We/They substitute He/She/It substitutes **Past:** substituted		• **Nouns:** substitute, substitution

Verbal Practice

Talk about It   **Read** each sentence and **think** about how you would complete it.

Discuss your idea with your partner using the sentence frame.

Listen carefully to your partner's and classmates' ideas.

Write your favorite idea in the blank.

❶ Because I want to eat healthier food, I have **substituted** _____ for my usual snack.

❷ When I hurt my knee, I **substituted** _____ for running in order to stay fit.

Writing Practice

Collaborate **Work with your partner** to complete the sentence using the correct form of **substitute** and appropriate content.

If scientists found a way to _____ seawater for _____ , they

would be able to _____ .

Your Turn **Work independently** to complete the sentence using the correct form of **substitute** and appropriate content.

In my writing, I frequently _____ boring, _____

words with _____ words.

Be an Academic Author **Work independently** to write two sentences. In your first sentence, use **substitute** in the *present perfect tense*. In your second sentence, use **substitute** with the adverb of frequency *frequently*.

❶ _____

_____

❷ _____

_____

> ### grammar tip
>
> **The present perfect tense is formed with *has/have* + the past participle form of the verb. To make the past participle of regular verbs, add *–d* or *–ed*.**
>
> She has substitute**d** initials for full names.
>
> He has play**ed** the piano for years.

Write an Academic Paragraph **Complete** the paragraph using the correct form of **substitute** and original content.

Vegetarians are people who do not eat _____ .
❶

Meat is a good source of protein, which is necessary for good health. However, vegetarians

can _____ plant-based protein for the protein found in meat. To get
❷

enough protein, vegetarians frequently _____ beans and nuts for
❸

meat. One cup of beans contains about 16 grams of _____ . Does
❹

becoming a _____ seem too difficult? Some families start with
❺

"Meatless Mondays." For one night, they _____ a vegetarian dinner,
❻

such as spaghetti or _____ , for a meal made with meat. It can be an
❼

easy way to try out vegetarianism.

sufficient

adjective

Say it: suf • **fi** • cient

Write it: _____

Academic Vocabulary Toolkit

Meaning	Example
enough of something *Antonym:* insufficient	When you go _____, make sure you bring **sufficient** _____ .

Family

- *Verb:* suffice
- *Noun:* sufficiency
- *Adverb:* sufficiently

Word Partners

• _____ evidence	The principal had **sufficient evidence** to suspend the students for vandalism.
• provide _____	Our teacher **provided sufficient** time for us to write our reports.

Verbal Practice

Talk about It   **Read** each sentence and **think** about how you would complete it.

Discuss your idea with your partner using the sentence frame.

Listen carefully to your partner's and classmates' ideas.

Write your favorite idea in the blank.

❶ I think a **sufficient** amount of time for a vocabulary quiz is

_____ minutes.

❷ One large pizza is **sufficient** to feed _____ .

Writing Practice

Collaborate   **Work with your partner** to complete the sentence using **sufficient** and appropriate content.

If students show _____ interest, the school will offer

_____ .

Your Turn   **Work independently** to complete the sentence using **sufficient** and appropriate content.

This new study provides _____ proof of a link between

_____ and _____ .

Be an Academic Author   **Work independently** to write two sentences. In your first sentence, use **sufficient** with the word partner *provide sufficient*. In your second sentence, use **sufficient** with the word partner *sufficient evidence*.

❶ _____

_____

❷ _____

_____

> ### grammar tip
> An adjective usually comes before the noun it describes.
>
> a <u>sufficient</u> amount
>
> a <u>big</u> house
>
> a <u>green</u> jacket

Write an Academic Paragraph   **Complete** the paragraph using **sufficient** and original content.

Sleep is an important part of good health. Experts say teens should get nine

_____ of sleep each night. Few teens, however, get a
　　　　　　　❶

_____ amount of sleep. Lack of _____ puts
　　　　　　　❷　　　　　　　　　　　　　　　　　❸

teens at risk for many health issues. If you do not get _____ sleep,
　　　　　　　　　　　　　　　　　　　　　　　　❹

you increase your chances of having an accident. You are more likely to get sick or develop an

_____ . Lack of sleep also contributes to acne and to weight gain. To help
　　　　　❺

yourself get sufficient sleep, don't have any coffee or _____ after 4:00 P.M.
　　　　　　　　　　　　　　　　　　　　　　　❻

One hour before you want to sleep, turn off your TV, _____ , and cell
　　　　　　　　　　　　　　　　　　　　　　　❼

phone. Remember, getting _____ sleep is a fundamental part of
　　　　　　　　　　　❽

good health.

summarize
verb

▶ *Say it:* **sum • ma • rize**   *Write it:* _____

Meaning	Example	
to give only the most important information about something or someone	Leon's _____ **summarizes** important _____ in the Civil War.	**IMPORTANT CIVIL WAR BATTLES** July 1861 — Battle of Bull Run March 1862 — Monitor vs. Merrimac September 1862 — Antietam July 1863 — Vicksburg July 1863 — Gettysburg

Forms	Family
Present: I/You/We/They summarize He/She/It summarizes **Past:** summarized	• **Noun:** summary

Word Partners	
• briefly _____	At the beginning of each chapter, the author **briefly summarizes** the contents.
• _____ the results	For the science fair, we **summarized the results** of our study on a poster.

Verbal Practice

Talk about It **Read** each sentence and **think** about how you would complete it.

Discuss your idea with your partner using the sentence frame.

Listen carefully to your partner's and classmates' ideas.

Write your favorite idea in the blank.

❶ Don't tell me every detail of _____ ; just briefly **summarize** the main points.

❷ I think it's boring when someone **summarizes** _____ for me.

Writing Practice

Collaborate   **Work with your partner** to complete the sentence using the correct form of **summarize** and appropriate content.

Jenna _____ her day in her _____ .

Your Turn   **Work independently** to complete the sentence using the correct form of **summarize** and appropriate content.

This newspaper headline _____ the results of last night's game:

_____ .

Be an Academic Author   **Work independently** to write two sentences. In your first sentence, use **summarize** in the *simple present tense* with *a person's name*. In your second sentence, use **summarize** in the *simple past tense* and include a word partner.

❶ _____

_____

❷ _____

_____

> **grammar tip**
>
> **In the simple present tense, the third person (*he/she/it*) form takes an –s or –es ending.**
>
> Malik summarizes his day in his diary.
>
> Mr. Tom teaches my biology class.

Write an Academic Paragraph   **Complete** the paragraph using the correct form of **summarize** and original content.

   The ability to take a lot of information and _____ it is an important
                                                            ❶

skill. Luckily, it is a _____ that you already use all the time. If someone
                              ❷

asks what you did today, you will probably answer, "I went to _____ ." If
                                                                              ❸

you didn't summarize, you might say, "I woke up, I got out of bed, I _____ ;"
                                                                                  ❹

and on and on. This is much more _____ than is necessary!
                                            ❺

Similarly, when your friend asks you about a movie or a book, you will probably

_____ it in one or two sentences. When you tell your parents about a test
            ❻

that you took, you give them a quick summary: "It was about state capitals" or "It was a test on

_____ ." If we didn't _____ , we'd have a lot less
            ❼   ❽

time to do what we want.

summary
noun

▶ **Say it:** **sum** • ma • ry   *Write it:* _____

Meaning	Example
a short statement of the most important features of an event or work	The last _____ provided a _____ **summary** of the presentation.

Forms	Family
• *Singular:* summary • *Plural:* summaries	• *Verb:* summarize

Word Partners

• brief _____	My sister told us a **brief summary** of the movie so we could decide if we wanted to see it.
• _____ of the results	The newspaper printed a **summary of the results** of the school committee meeting.
• provide a _____	The author **provides a summary** at the end of every chapter.

Verbal Practice

Talk about It **Read** each sentence and **think** about how you would complete it.

Discuss your idea with your partner using the sentence frame.

Listen carefully to your partner's and classmates' ideas.

Write your favorite idea in the blank.

❶ Teachers ask students to write **summaries** to find out if

_____ .

❷ In a brief **summary**, you should include only the _____ .

Writing Practice

Collaborate **Work with your partner** to complete the sentence using the correct form of **summary** and appropriate content.

In the back of the book, there are _____ of the results of all of the

_____ .

Your Turn **Work independently** to complete the sentence using the correct form of **summary** and appropriate content.

For history, I prepared a _____ of the _____ ,

including how it started.

Be an Academic Author **Work independently** to write two sentences. In your first sentence, use **summary** in the *singular form* and include a word partner. In your second sentence, use **summary** in the *plural form*.

❶ _____

_____

❷ _____

_____

> ### grammar tip
> To form the plural of count nouns that end in a consonant + *y*, change the *y* to *i* and add *–es*.
>
> summary—summar**ies**
> party—part**ies**

Write an Academic Paragraph **Complete** the paragraph using the correct form of **summary** and original content.

William Shakespeare wrote 37 _____ ❶ . If each play takes three hours

to watch (and some take longer), it would take over _____ ❷ hours

to see every play. But now, thanks to the Reduced Shakespeare Company, you can see a

97-minute _____ ❸ that includes every play Shakespeare wrote! *The

Complete Works of William Shakespeare (abridged)* is a comic _____ ❹

of Shakespeare's plays. Actors take only four _____ ❺ to perform their

very funny summary of Act I of *Romeo and Juliet*. The entire _____ ❻

of *Othello*, which is performed as a rap, takes three minutes. But if you get a chance to

see *The Complete Works of William Shakespeare (abridged),* you won't be looking at your

_____ ❼ . You'll be too busy laughing.

symbol
noun

▶ **Say it:** **sym** • bol

Write it: _____

Meaning	Example
something that is used to represent something else	Oscar gave Jennifer a _____ roses as a **symbol** of his _____ .
Synonym: sign	

Forms	Family
• *Singular:* symbol • *Plural:* symbols	• *Noun:* symbolism • *Verb:* symbolize • *Adjective:* symbolic • *Adverb:* symbolically

Word Partners

• become a _____	Sunglasses have **become a symbol** of fame, but they also serve a serious purpose.
• status _____	**Status symbols** like mansions and expensive cars represent success to some people.
• universal _____	A white dove is the **universal symbol** of peace.

Verbal Practice

Talk about It **Read** each sentence and **think** about how you would complete it.

Discuss your idea with your partner using the sentence frame.

Listen carefully to your partner's and classmates' ideas.

Write your favorite idea in the blank.

❶ A _____ has become a **symbol** of
_____ .

❷ One status **symbol** that I would like to have is a _____ .

Writing Practice

Collaborate **Work with your partner** to complete the sentence using the correct form of **symbol** and appropriate content.

Signs in airports and train stations often use universal _____ , such as a

_____ to mean _____ .

Your Turn **Work independently** to complete the sentence using the correct form of **symbol** and appropriate content.

On a computer _____ , you need to use the shift key to type many

_____ , such as the dollar sign and the _____ .

Be an Academic Author **Work independently** to write two sentences. In your first sentence, use **symbol** in the *singular form* and include a word partner. In your second sentence, use **symbol** in the *plural form* with the quantifier *many*.

❶ _____

_____

❷ _____

_____

> ### grammar tip
>
> Quantifiers are words that tell us how much or how many of something there is. They usually come before the noun they describe.
>
> I use **many symbols** when I text.
>
> He has **a few ideas** for our project.

Write an Academic Paragraph **Complete** the paragraph using the correct form of **symbol** and original content.

Ancient Egyptians used hieroglyphs in their art and writing. A hieroglyph is a picture

that serves as a _____ for a word or an idea. Elaborately painted
❶

_____ and lines of hieroglyphic writing on temple walls tell
❷

_____ of gods and pharaohs, battles, and daily life. Some hieroglyphs
❸

represent abstract _____ . For example, a lotus plant symbolizes Upper
❹

Egypt, and a papyrus plant symbolizes Lower _____ . The two symbols
❺

often appear together in art to _____ the unification of the two lands.
❻

Egyptian _____ also used hieroglyphs to represent phonetic sounds,
❼

much like letters in the English _____ .
❽

189

symbolize
verb

Say it: **sym** • bol • ize   *Write it:* _____

Academic Vocabulary Toolkit

Meaning	Example
to represent something *Synonym:* represent	The gold cross in the flag of _____ **symbolizes** sunlight and the country's natural _____ .

Forms	Family
Present: I/You/We/They symbolize He/She/It symbolizes *Past:* symbolized	• **Nouns:** symbol, symbolism • **Adjective:** symbolic • **Adverb:** symbolically

Word Partners	
• come to _____	Ribbons of different colors have **come to symbolize** different causes.
• meant to _____	Cutting the cake at a wedding is **meant to symbolize** the bride and groom working together.

Verbal Practice

Talk about It   **Read** each sentence and **think** about how you would complete it.

Discuss your idea with your partner using the sentence frame.

Listen carefully to your partner's and classmates' ideas.

Write your favorite idea in the blank.

❶ The color red sometimes **symbolizes** _____ .

❷ I think that _____ has come to **symbolize** the United States for people around the world.

Writing Practice

Collaborate Work with your partner to complete the sentence using the correct form of **symbolize** and appropriate content.

My _____ wristband is meant to _____

my support of _____ .

Your Turn Work independently to complete the sentence using the correct form of **symbolize** and appropriate content.

Animals in folk tales often _____ human traits; for example, a

_____ sometimes _____

the human characteristic of _____ .

Be an Academic Author Work independently to write two sentences. In your first sentence, use **symbolize** with a word partner. In your second sentence, use **symbolize** in the *present tense* with the adverb of frequency *often*.

❶ _____

_____

❷ _____

_____

> ### grammar tip
>
> **Adverbs of frequency are words that show how often something happens. They usually go before the main verb.**
>
> An owl **often** symbolizes wisdom.
>
> We **usually order** pizza on Friday nights.

Write an Academic Paragraph **Complete** the paragraph using the correct form of **symbolize** and original content.

In 1942, a young Jewish man named Pavel Friedman was _____
❶

at Terezin, a Nazi concentration camp. There, he wrote a poem called "The Butterfly,"

about the only _____ he ever saw in the camp. For Friedman,
❷

this butterfly _____ hope, innocence, beauty, life, and freedom.
❸

_____ , Friedman died in another concentration camp two years
❹

after writing "The Butterfly." In 2008, a museum in Houston began the Butterfly Project, whose

_____ was to collect 1.5 million paper _____
❺   ❻

from schoolchildren. The butterflies would _____ the 1.5 million children
❼

killed during the Nazi Holocaust.

transition
noun

Say it: tran • **si** • tion

Write it: _____

Academic Vocabulary Toolkit

Meaning	Example
a change from one thing to another **Synonyms:** shift, switch	Over the course of a year, we watched Boots go through the **transition** from a _____ kitten to a _____ adult cat.

Forms	Family
• **Singular:** transition • **Plural:** transitions	• **Verb:** transition • **Adjective:** transitional

Word Partners

• difficult _____	For the Kwan family, moving from Shanghai to Cincinnati was a **difficult transition**.
• period of _____	There was a brief **period of transition** between the old and new governments.
• smooth _____	Colleges work hard to help students make a **smooth transition** from high school.

Verbal Practice

Talk about It **Read** each sentence and **think** about how you would complete it.

Discuss your idea with your partner using the sentence frame.

Listen carefully to your partner's and classmates' ideas.

Write your favorite idea in the blank.

❶ Going through the **transition** from _____ to

_____ can be challenging.

❷ Using words like *at first*, *generally*, and _____ in your writing

can help you make smooth **transitions** from one point to another.

Writing Practice

Collaborate   **Work with your partner** to complete the sentence using the correct form of **transition** and appropriate content.

I see the teen years as a period of _____ between

_____ and _____ .

Your Turn   **Work independently** to complete the sentence using the correct form of **transition** and appropriate content.

For some countries, the difficult _____ from

_____ to _____ can result in a war.

Be an Academic Author   **Work independently** to write two sentences. In your first sentence, use **transition** in the *singular form*. In your second sentence, use **transition** in the *plural form*. Use a word partner in one of your sentences.

❶ _____

_____

❷ _____

_____

> ### grammar tip
> An adjective usually comes before the noun it describes.
>
> a **difficult** transition
>
> **healthy** meals

Write an Academic Paragraph   **Complete** the paragraph using the correct form of **transition** and original content.

Do you forget your dreams as soon as you wake up? It's easy to forget dreams during

that hazy period of _____ between sleep and wakefulness.
     ❶

However, if you keep a _____ next to your bed, you can record
           ❷

everything that you remember as soon as you _____ . Then you
             ❸

can try to analyze your dreams. When you _____ a dream, you try
           ❹

to figure out what the dream means. Dreams can reflect what a person is going through

in real life. If you are going through a difficult _____ in life, you
            ❺

might dream of going over a bridge or waiting at a train station. Dreaming that you are

being chased by _____ may mean that you are under a lot of
        ❻

_____ in real life.
    ❼

trend
noun

Write it: _____

Meaning	Example
a general change toward something different **Synonyms:** tendency, style	Last year continued a **trend** of _____ global temperatures.

RISE IN EARTH'S TEMPERATURE 1880 - 2020

Forms	Family
• **Singular:** trend • **Plural:** trends	• **Verb:** trend • **Adjective:** trendy

Word Partners

• _____ toward	Recently, there is a **trend toward** serving healthier foods in school cafeterias.
• continue the _____	Last night the basketball team **continued the trend** it started last week and won another game.
• reverse the _____	The price of gold went down, **reversing the trend** of recent months.

Verbal Practice

Talk about It **Read** each sentence and **think** about how you would complete it.

Discuss your idea with your partner using the sentence frame.

Listen carefully to your partner's and classmates' ideas.

Write your favorite idea in the blank.

❶ Among teenagers there is a **trend** toward

_____ .

❷ We have to do something to reverse the **trend** of

_____ .

Writing Practice

Collaborate Work with your partner to complete the sentence using the correct form of **trend** and appropriate content.

Current _____ in movies include movies about

_____ or _____ .

Your Turn Work independently to complete the sentence using the correct form of **trend** and appropriate content.

Our school hopes to continue the _____ of increasing numbers of

students _____ .

Be an Academic Author Work independently to write two sentences. In your first sentence, use **trend** in the *singular form*. In your second sentence, use **trend** in the *plural form* and include a word partner.

❶ _____

_____

❷ _____

_____

> ### grammar tip
>
> Count nouns name things that be counted. Count nouns have two forms, singular and plural. To make most count nouns plural, add −s.
>
> She doesn't follow popular trends in music.
>
> He likes board games.

Write an Academic Paragraph Complete the paragraph using the correct form of **trend** and original content.

In fashion there are people who start _____ ❶ , people who

follow them, and people who completely _____ ❷ them. A

trendsetter is someone with a strong personality and lots of charisma and charm.

People _____ ❸ and want to be like that person, so they begin

_____ ❹ some aspect of the person's style—maybe a haircut, an

accessory, or a way of _____ ❺ . Then the _____ ❻

spreads and can soon be seen everywhere. Some people choose to stay away from any kind

of fashion _____ ❼ . They value their own personal style over whatever is

_____ ❽ at the moment. Which category do you belong to?

value
noun

Write it: _____

Academic Vocabulary Toolkit

Meanings	Examples
1. how useful or important something is; what something is worth	1. Although it only cost a few _____ dollars, Katie's old _____ was of great **value** to her.
2. beliefs about what is right and wrong or what is important **Synonyms:** principle, belief	2. Kirk's _____ **values** led him to tell the _____ to his mother.

Forms	Family
• **Singular:** value • **Plural:** values	• **Verb:** value • **Adjective:** valuable, valued

Word Partners	
• actual _____ • increase in _____	The **actual value** of this ring is low, but it means everything to me. When you buy a stock, you hope it will **increase in value**.

Verbal Practice

Talk about It **Read** each sentence and **think** about how you would complete it.

Discuss your idea with your partner using the sentence frame.

Listen carefully to your partner's and classmates' ideas.

Write your favorite idea in the blank.

❶ My _____ is of great **value** to me.

❷ You can't put a price on the **value** of _____ .

❸ Respect for others and _____ are important **values**.

❹ People in different _____ often have different **values**.

Writing Practice

Collaborate **Work with your partner** to complete the sentences using the correct form of **value** and appropriate content.

❶ Years from now, _____ will have increased in _____ .

❷ I learned my most important _____ at _____ .

Your Turn **Work independently** to complete the sentences using the correct form of **value** and appropriate content.

❶ The _____ of a college education includes not only a higher income but also

_____ .

❷ My _____ and I share many common _____ .

Be an Academic Author **Work independently** to write two sentences. In your first sentence, use **value** in the *singular form* and include a word partner. In your second sentence, use **value** in the *plural form*.

MEANING ❶ _____

_____

MEANING ❷ _____

_____

> ### grammar tip
>
> **Meaning 1 of *value* is a non-count noun. Non-count nouns have only one form. Do not add an –*s* to a non-count noun.**
>
> The **value** of those paintings has increased.
>
> The **water** in the lake is frozen.

Write an Academic Paragraph **Complete** the paragraph using the correct form of **value** and original content.

Many schools these day place a much higher _____ on
                    ❶

math and science than on the arts. However, some educators argue that a well-rounded

_____ also needs to study art and _____ .
        ❷   ❸

Studies show that music in particular has more than just artistic _____ .
                                                       ❹

Music education improves students' _____ in other subject
                                    ❺

areas, including reading and math. Music can add to students' creativity and problem-

solving _____ , which help them do better on tests. Students
                    ❻

involved in music education are also more likely to stay in school. They appreciate the

_____ of the arts in education.
        ❼

version
noun

▶ **Say it:** **ver** • sion   **Write it:** _____

Academic Vocabulary Toolkit

Meaning	Example
a form of something that is different from other forms of the same thing	After several _____ , Andrea turned in the final **version** of her _____ .

Forms

- *Singular:* version
- *Plural:* versions

Word Partners

• original _____	A new version of the movie *Clash of the Titans* came out in 2010, but the **original version** came out in 1981.
• updated _____	The game isn't working because you don't have the **updated version** of Flash installed on your computer.

Verbal Practice

Talk about It   **Read** each sentence and **think** about how you would complete it.

Discuss your idea with your partner using the sentence frame.

Listen carefully to your partner's and classmates' ideas.

Write your favorite idea in the blank.

❶ I prefer to play the original **version** of _____ .

❷ I have heard many different **versions** of the song _____ .

Writing Practice

Collaborate | **Work with your partner** to complete the sentence using the correct form of **version** and appropriate content.

I downloaded the updated _____ of _____ for

_____ .

Your Turn | **Work independently** to complete the sentence using the correct form of **version** and appropriate content.

I had to write several _____ of _____ before I

_____ .

Be an Academic Author | **Work independently** to write two sentences. In your first sentence, use **version** in the *singular form* and include a word partner. In your second sentence, use **version** in the *plural form* with the quantifier *several*.

❶ _____

_____

❷ _____

_____

> ### grammar tip
>
> **Quantifiers are words that tell us how much or how many of something there is. They usually come before the noun they describe.**
>
> I have heard **several versions** of that song.
>
> This store sells **various brands** of clothes.

Write an Academic Paragraph | **Complete** the paragraph using the correct form of **version** and original content.

It can be _____❶_____ to keep up with new technology these days.

Tech companies are always releasing new, improved _____❷_____ of

their software and of devices such as computers and _____❸_____ . New

_____❹_____ are always added to make the item very appealing. A computer

or phone that is just a few years old can be considered _____❺_____ ! Many

people feel pressured to buy the latest _____❻_____ of everything. This

can be very _____❼_____ . So what is the solution? You can try holding

on to your old devices and looking for free software downloads. Or, you can get an extra

_____❽_____ to pay for all of your upgrades!

viewpoint
noun

▶ **Say it:** **view** • point   ***Write it:*** _____

Meaning	Example
the way someone thinks about something	If high school students are _____ in expressing their **viewpoints**, they should consider joining the _____ club.
Synonyms: view, opinion	

Forms

- *Singular:* viewpoint
- *Plural:* viewpoints

Word Partners

- express a _____   In his book, he **expresses a viewpoint** which not everyone agrees with.
- particular _____   Most novels are told from one **particular viewpoint**.

Verbal Practice

Talk about It **Read** each sentence and **think** about how you would complete it.

Discuss your idea with your partner using the sentence frame.

Listen carefully to your partner's and classmates' ideas.

Write your favorite idea in the blank.

❶ On the show _____ , people feel free to express their **viewpoints**.

❷ I would enjoy reading a story told from the **viewpoints** of several different _____ .

200

Writing Practice

Collaborate   Work with your partner to complete the sentence using the correct form of **viewpoint** and appropriate content.

From the _____ of a student attending this school, I would say that the school

needs to put more funding into the _____ program.

Your Turn   Work independently to complete the sentence using the correct form of **viewpoint** and appropriate content.

If you only look at things from one particular _____ , you might not

_____

Be an Academic Author   Work independently to write two sentences. In your first sentence, use **viewpoint** in the *singular form* and include a word partner. In your second sentence, use **viewpoint** in the *plural form* with the quantifier *a variety of*.

❶ _____

_____

❷ _____

_____

grammar tip

Quantifiers are words that tell us how much or how many of something there is. They usually come before the noun they describe.

Look at different Web sites to get **a variety of** viewpoints.

There are **numerous mistakes** in your paper.

Write an Academic Paragraph   Complete the paragraph using the correct form of **viewpoint** and original content.

Originally, blogs were called Web logs. A log is another word for journal, and a blog

is similar to a _____ ❶ . However, instead of expressing your

_____ ❷ in your personal journal, you can publish them for the

world to see! Every blog is a little bit different, partly because every blogger has a different

_____ ❸ . Bloggers voice their _____ ❹ on varied

topics such as politics, computer games, or _____ ❺ . Many blogs have

a comment section, where readers can _____ ❻ comments, much like

teachers give _____ ❼ on papers. Through the comments, readers can

justify their own particular _____ ❽ or just agree with the ideas in the blog.

Photo Credits

p. **2:** © Mel Yates/Getty images; p. **4:** © Heiko Kiera/Shutterstock; p. **6:** top, © Hill Street Studios/Blend Images/Corbis p. **6:** bottom, © Paul Orr/Shutterstock; p. **8:** © Dustie/Shutterstock; p. **10:** left, © DElight/iStockphoto p. **10:** right, © Jandrie Lombard/Shutterstock; p. **12:** © Don Romero/Age fotostock; p. **14:** © Mark Evans/iStockphoto; p. **16:** © Marco Baroncini/Corbis; p. **18:** © Carlos Barria/Reuters/Corbis; p. **20:** © ZoneCreative/iStockphoto; p. **24:** © Monkey Business Images/Shutterstock; p. **26:** © Twindesigner | Dreamstime.com; p. **28:** top, © Digital Vision/Thinkstock p. **28:** bottom, © auremar/Shutterstock; p. **30:** © George Doyle/Thinkstock; p. **34:** © juan carlos tinjaca/Shutterstock; p. **36:** © Artem Kursin/Shutterstock; p. **42:** © Fuse/Getty Images; p. **50:** bottom left, © Allstar Picture Library/Alamy p. **50:** bottom right, © Christopher Halloran/Shutterstock p. **50:** top, © Fenton one/Shutterstock; p. **52:** © Photobac/Shutterstock; p. **62:** © Monkey Business Images/Shutterstock; p. **66:** © Joel Gordon; p. **68:** © MARC ROMANELLI/Alamy; p. **70:** © ansar80/Shutterstock; p. **72:** © Ilene MacDonald/Alamy; p. **80:** © dny3d/Shutterstock; p. **82:** © Dušan Kosti#/iStockphoto; p. **84:** © Adam Gryko/Shutterstock; p. **86:** © Stephen Coburn/Shutterstock; p. **96:** top, © FETHI BELAID/AFP/Getty Images p. **96:** bottom, © MOHAMMED HOSSAM/AFP/Getty Images; p. **98:** © Christopher Futcher/iStockphoto; p. **102:** © doglikehorse/Shutterstock; p. **104:** © Ryan Ruffatti/iStockphoto; p. **106:** top, © Mara Susanna Marucci/iStockphoto; p. **108:** © thieury/Shutterstock; p. **110:** © Yuri Arcurs/Shutterstock; p. **116:** © Bettmann/CORBIS; p. **118:** © AP Images/Nati Harnik; p. **120:** © Tyler Olson/Shutterstock; p. **122:** bottom, © GoodMood Photo/Shutterstock p. **122:** top, © kojoku/Shutterstock; p. **124:** © Veronika Mannova/Shutterstock; p. **130:** © Ben Blankenburg/iStockphoto; p. **134:** © Robert J. Beyers II/Shutterstock; p. **136:** © Thinkstock; p. **138:** © Mark Herreid/Shutterstock; p. **140:** © Golden Pixels LLC/Alamy; p. **142:** © Chris Schmidt/iStockphoto; p. **144:** © Neustockimages/iStockphoto; p. **150:** © Aleksandra Yakovleva/iStockphoto; p. **154:** © pjcross/Shutterstock; p. **158:** bottom, © Jeff Greenberg/Alamy; p. **162:** top, © krechet/Shutterstock; p. **164:** top, © Lisa F. Young/Shutterstock; p. **166:** top, © Linda Bucklin/Shutterstock; p. **168:** © Kochneva Tetyana/Shutterstock; p. **174:** © Slobodan Vasic/iStockphoto; p. **176:** © GoGo Images Corporation/Alamy; p. **178:** © Comstock/Thinkstock; p. **180:** © PAUL ELLIS/Getty Images; p. **182:** © Alexander Ishchenko/Shutterstock; p. **186:** © Keith Morris/Age fotostock; p. **190:** © Fenton/Shutterstock; p. **196:** top, © Michelle Marsan/Shutterstock p. **196:** bottom, © Thinkstock; p. **200:** © Bob Daemmrich/PhotoEdit

Grammar Lessons

Singular Nouns and the Simple Present Tense

Sample Sentences

❶ Broccoli contains a lot of vitamins.

❷ She listens to her messages before lunch.

❸ Elena babysits her little brother on Tuesdays while her mother goes to yoga class.

❹ My cousin believes in UFOs.

Simple Present Tense

The simple present tense has two forms: the base form and the –s form.

Subject	Verb
I You We They	read.
He/She/It	reads.

Singular Nouns and the Simple Present Tense

- Singular means "one." A singular noun is one of something: a book, Wendy Brown, the school, Miami.

- In the simple present, use the –s form of the verb when the subject is a singular noun or *he, she,* or *it*. This is called the "third-person singular."

Spelling Changes in the Simple Present Tense

- When the base form of the verb ends in *s, sh, ch,* or *x*, add –es.

- When the base form of the verb ends in a consonant + *y*, change the *y* to *i* and add –es.

- Add –es to *go* and *do*.

- *Have* is irregular. The –s form of *have* is *has*.

Base Form	–s Form
kiss	kiss**es**
catch	catch**es**
fix	fix**es**
cry	cries
go	go**es**
have	has

Collaborate **Work with your partner** to complete the sentences using the simple present tense form of each verb and original content.

1 make

In our class, _____ is the student who

_____ everyone laugh.

2 go/listen

During lunch, _____ , the principal of our

school, _____ to the nurse's office and

_____ to hip-hop music.

3 try/act

A good student always _____

his or her best and _____ respectfully.

4 mix

Leo often _____ together condiments

like _____ and _____ and eats

them with french fries.

5 have

At least one student in this class _____ a

problem understanding _____ .

Your Turn **Work independently** to complete the sentences using the simple present tense form of each verb.

1 watch

Every night, Kayla _____ about three hours

of TV.

2 want

He _____ his parents to buy a new car.

3 pass/say

When she _____ me in the hall, she never

_____ anything.

4 go/do

My sister _____ into the bathroom every

morning and _____ her hair for about

an hour!

5 think/crush

He _____ he's so strong when he

_____ a soda can.

Plural Forms of Nouns

Sample Sentences

1. Most teachers arrive at school before 7:00 a.m.
2. Some classes have over 30 students.
3. Zhi went to the store to buy potatoes and tomatoes.
4. All the babies in the hospital were boys.

Forms of Plural Nouns

- To form the plural of most count nouns, add –s to the singular form.
- To form the plural of nouns that end in ss, ch, sh, or x, add –es.
- To form the plural of nouns that end in a consonant + y, change the y to i and add –es.
- To form the plural of most nouns that end in a consonant + o, add –es.
- Some singular nouns that end in –is form the plural by changing the –is to –es.
- Some nouns have irregular plural forms.

Singular	Plural
animal	animals
kiss	kisses
peach	peaches
box	boxes
party	parties
echo	echoes
crisis	crises
child	children

Collaborate Work with your partner to complete the sentences using the correct form of each noun.

1. penguin — On our field trip to the zoo, we saw dozens of _____ .
2. potato/ strawberry — My favorite foods include mashed _____ and _____ .
3. eye — Selena drew a picture of a monster with four _____ .
4. skirt — In our class, three people are wearing _____ .
5. inch — Cesar is five feet nine _____ tall.

Your Turn Work independently to complete the sentences using the correct form of each noun.

1. house — On my street, three _____ are painted white.
2. church — There are several _____ in my neighborhood.
3. hero — Many brave _____ died in World War II.
4. lady — In the past, some _____ wore long skirts.
5. child — Dozens of _____ are playing in the park.

Quantifiers

Sample Sentences

1. None of the books on the reading list are in the library.
2. A superhero fights for both truth and justice.
3. Many people in this class speak Mandarin.
4. Take a lot of food and water when you go camping.

Placement of Quantifiers

- Quantifiers are words or expressions that tell how much or how many of a noun there is.

- Quantifiers go before the noun and before adjectives describing the noun.

- We use quantifiers with count and non-count nouns. Some quantifiers can only be used with count nouns.

Quantifier	Count	Non-count
no	x	x
none of	x	
both	x	x
a few	x	
several	x	
a lot of	x	x
a number of	x	
many	x	
numerous	x	

Collaborate **Work with a partner** to complete the sentences using appropriate quantifiers and original content.

1. In our class, _____ students want to become _____ .

2. Mario went _____ and broke _____ his legs.

3. _____ the movies at my local theater sound _____ .

4. Jordan found _____ pencils at the bottom of her _____ .

5. Last night my _____ baked _____ cookies.

Your Turn **Work independently** to complete the sentences using appropriate quantifiers and original content.

1. There are _____ televisions in my _____ .

2. My dream house has _____ _____ .

3. On the test, _____ the possible answers to the first question seemed _____ .

4. You need to take _____ classes in science and _____ if you want to graduate.

5. I like to drink _____ with _____ sugar.

Simple Past Tense of Regular Verbs

1. Yesterday at the football game, Franco kicked the winning field goal.

2. I moved to the United States from Haiti ten years ago.

3. My dad fried catfish for dinner last night.

4. We shopped at that store every week until it closed.

Simple Past Tense of Regular Verbs

- The form of the simple past tense is the same for all persons.

- To form the simple past tense of most regular verbs, add –ed to the base form of the verb.

Base Form	Simple Past Tense
listen	listen**ed**
start	start**ed**
open	open**ed**
want	want**ed**

- Add –d to regular verbs that end in e.

- For verbs that end in a consonant + y, change the y to i and add –ed.

- Some verbs that end in a consonant form the past tense by doubling the final consonant and then adding –ed.

Base Form	Simple Past Tense
smile	smil**ed**
cry	cri**ed**
permit	permit**ted**

Collaborate **Work with your partner** to complete the sentences using the simple past tense form of each verb and original content.

① sub

Last week, when our _____ teacher was sick, _____ _____ for her.

② ask/cook

My mother _____ me to make dinner, so I _____ my favorite meal: _____ .

③ carry

Because it was so heavy, I _____ my grandmother's _____ upstairs for her.

④ die/pass/crash

We almost _____ last night when a car _____ us on the right and _____ into us.

⑤ attend

All the students _____ the _____ .

Your Turn **Work independently** to complete the sentences using the simple past tense form of each verb.

① wait

Yesterday I _____ at the bus stop for over an hour.

② occur

Over 25 years ago, a nuclear disaster _____ in Europe.

③ worry

Before she took the test, Jill _____ that she might fail.

④ live

Shakespeare _____ in England from 1564 to 1616.

⑤ admit/rob

The criminal finally _____ that he _____ the bank last week.

Present Progressive Tense

Sample Sentences

❶ We are studying vocabulary.

❷ I am listening to music at the moment.

❸ Mr. Ortiz is losing weight because he is exercising every day.

❹ Look, it is raining.

Forms of the Present Progressive Tense

The present progressive tense is formed with *am/is/are* and a verb ending in –*ing*.

Subject	*be*	Verb + –*ing*
I	am	reading.
You/We/They	are	studying.
He/She/It	is	laughing.

Uses of the Present Progressive Tense

- Use the present progressive tense for an action that is happening right now.
- Use the present progressive tense to show a long-term action that is in progress.
- We do not usually use the present progressive tense with nonaction verbs like *seem, see, like, know,* and *want*. For example, we do not say: *I am liking the weather.*

Spelling Changes

- If the verb ends in a consonant + *e*, drop the *e* before adding –*ing*.
- For a one-syllable verb that ends in a consonant + vowel + consonant (CVC), double the final consonant and add –*ing*.
- Do not double a final *w, x,* or *y*.
- For a two-syllable verb that ends in a CVC, double the final consonant only if the last syllable is stressed.

Verb	–*ing* Form
dance	dancing
stop	stopping
stay	staying
permit	permitting
offer	offering

Collaborate **Work with your partner** to complete the sentences using the present progressive form of each verb and original content.

1 wear   Tanya's clothes are crazy; today she _____ purple

shoes and _____ .

2 shop   I _____ for a new _____ for next

week's _____ .

3 bake   My mother _____ a cake for

_____ .

4 begin   To prepare for their trip to _____ , Alanna and Rob

_____ to study Spanish.

5 make   Many students _____ plans for

_____ .

Your Turn **Work independently** to complete the sentences using the present progressive form of each verb and original content.

1 sit   Today in class I _____ behind

_____ .

2 plan   My friends _____ a surprise party for

_____ .

3 stay   Hailey _____ after school today because she

_____ .

4 listen   In music class, the students _____ to the music of

_____ .

5 offer   This week the cafeteria _ _____ everyone a free

_____ .

Present Perfect Tense

Sample Sentences

❶ I have played football since I was seven.

❷ She has promised to help me with my essay.

❸ Sophia has already spoken to her parents about getting her driver's license.

❹ We have just finished eating lunch.

Forms of the Present Perfect Tense

Subject	*have/has*	Past Participle
I You We They	have	played.
He/She/It	has	promised.

- The present perfect tense is formed with *has/have* + the past participle form of the verb.
- To make the past participle of regular verbs, add *–ed* or *–d*.
- Use *have* with *I, you, we, they,* and plural nouns.
- Use *has* with *he, she, it,* and singular nouns.

When to Use the Simple Past or Present Perfect

- Use the **simple past tense** when the action started and finished in the past.
- Use the **present perfect tense** when the action began in the past but continues into the present.
- We often use the **present perfect** with time words such as *already, since, always,* and *never*.
- We can also use the **present perfect** to talk about the recent past. Words like *just* and *recently* show the recent past.
- We also use the **present perfect** to talk about repeated actions in the past if the action might occur again in the future.

Collaborate Work with your partner to complete the sentences using the present perfect form of each verb and original content.

❶ read   Every day this week we _____

                                  _____ poems in class.

❷ hear   Can you believe that she _____ never

                                  _____ of _____ ?

❸ live   How long _____ you _____ in

                                  your home?

❹ finish   I _____ just _____ reading

                                  _____ ; it's an amazing book.

❺ be   Where is _____ ? He _____

                                  _____ absent a lot recently.

Your Turn Work independently to complete the sentences using the present perfect form of each verb.

❶ work   My mother _____ _____ for the

                                  same company since 2005.

❷ go   I _____ already _____ to the

                                  principal's office many times.

❸ live   Martin _____ _____ in California

                                  for four years.

❹ fall   Tara keeps ice skating even though she _____

                                  _____ many times.

❺ return   Alberto _____ just _____ from

                                  visiting his cousins in Puerto Rico.

Adverbs of Frequency

Sample Sentences

❶ Marco never goes to the pool; he can't swim.

❷ I always study the night before a test.

❸ Tiana is frequently late for volleyball practice.

❹ Usually, I buy lunch at school.

Meanings of Adverbs of Frequency

Adverbs of frequency show how often something happens.

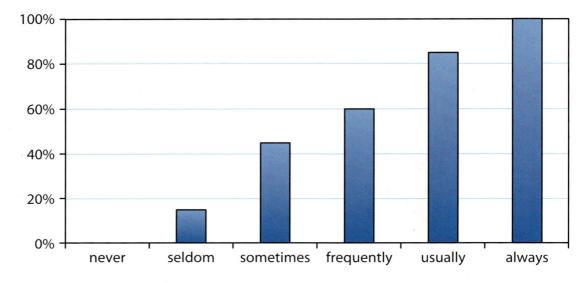

Placement of Adverbs of Frequency

• Adverbs of frequency come after the verb *be* but before other verbs.

• Adverbs of frequency go after a modal verb.

• Some adverbs of frequency, such as *usually, often, frequently, sometimes,* and *generally,* can also go at the beginning of a sentence.

Collaborate   **Work with your partner** to complete the sentences using appropriate adverbs of frequency and original content.

❶ I _____ brush my teeth before I _____ .

❷ Students in this class are _____ late because _____ .

❸ _____ , I have to agree with people who say _____ .

❹ When I see my _____ on the street, I _____ stop and talk to them.

❺ My family _____ goes to restaurants—maybe _____ times a _____ .

Your Turn   **Work independently** to complete the sentences using appropriate adverbs of frequency and original content.

❶ Now that I have _____ , I _____ watch TV.

❷ My brother loves his _____ . You _____ see him without it.

❸ She _____ gets a haircut; her hair is _____ .

❹ People in my family _____ speak _____ .

❺ _____ , I prefer to communicate with my friends by _____ .

Modal Verbs

Sample Sentences

1. If he has time, Kevin may help me move.
2. Mia can speak Russian, but she can't speak German.
3. If it rains, I might not go to the beach.
4. You should stay home and study tonight.

Modals: Form and Placement

- Modals do not have –s, –ed, or –ing endings.
- The base form of the verb follows the modal verb.
- Make modals negative by placing *not* right after the modal.

Modals and Their Meanings

Modal verbs give additional meaning to the main verb.

	Use	Example
can	ability request	Alex can walk on his hands. Can I talk to you later?
could	future possibility request past ability	This could end in a disaster. Could you speak more slowly? Once I could play the violin, but I've forgotten how.
may	permission future possibility	You may wait outside my office. Emilia may win a medal if she continues to practice.
might	possibility	If I ask nicely, my parents might let me have the car tonight.
must	obligation	Daniel must visit his grandmother on Sunday.
should	advice	You should eat more vegetables.
will	prediction promise	Coach thinks we will win the state championship this year. I will call you tomorrow.
would	preference invitation	I would like iced tea, please. Would you play tennis with me?

Collaborate Work with your partner to complete the sentences using appropriate modals and base forms of verbs and original content.

❶ During a test, you _____ not _____ .

❷ I promise I _____ _____ everything I can

to _____ .

❸ If you want to make the basketball team, you _____

_____ .

❹ My best friend _____ _____ very well, but I'm

hopeless!

❺ In the future, people _____ be able to _____ .

Your Turn Work independently to complete the sentences using appropriate modals and base forms of verbs and original content.

❶ I want to go to the _____ , but Jayden _____

_____ to go to the mall.

❷ Your _____ is so old; you _____

_____ a new one.

❸ I'm so busy—_____ you _____ this for me?

❹ Raul _____ _____ to Europe this summer, but he

doesn't want to.

❺ Zoe and I are going _____ ; _____ you like to come

with us?

Adjectives

Sample Sentences

❶ Every night my father cooks a healthy dinner.

❷ Look at the people walking down the busy streets.

❸ You should take a nap—you look sleepy.

❹ Last summer I read many fascinating novels.

Adjectives: Placement and Number

- An adjective describes a noun.

- An adjective usually comes before the noun it describes.

- Adjectives can come after the verb *be* and verbs like *look, sound, smell, taste,* and *feel.*

- Adjectives are always singular, even if they describe a plural noun. Do not add –*s* to adjectives that describe plural nouns.

Collaborate **Work with a partner** to complete the sentences using appropriate adjectives and original content.

❶ We watched a _____ sunset.

❷ After spending lots of money at the _____ , Sam has a _____ smile.

❸ The _____ smells _____ ; bring it outside.

❹ Russ and Amy are _____ musicians who play _____ .

❺ Canada and _____ are _____ countries.

Your Turn **Work independently** to complete the following sentences using appropriate adjectives and original content.

❶ I usually listen to music like _____ that is _____ and _____ .

❷ Jack and Devon are _____ guys who like baseball and _____ .

❸ This playground has _____ rides and is painted _____ colors.

❹ Deserts are _____ places.

❺ _____ is a/an _____ last name in _____ .